The Path of **Love**

THE *Mananam* SERIES

The Path of
Love

CHINMAYA PUBLICATIONS

Chinmaya Publications
Chinmaya Mission West Publications Division
Main Office
P.O. Box 129
Piercy, CA 95587, USA

Chinmaya Publications
Chinmaya Mission West Publications Division
Distribution Office
560 Bridgetown Pike
Langhorne, PA 19053, USA

Central Chinmaya Mission Trust
Sandeepany Sadhanalaya
Saki Vihar Road
Bombay, India 400 072

Credits:

Series Editors: Margaret Leuverink, Br. Rajeshwar, Lalita Shenoy
Front cover design and inside photographs: Treehouse Digital Studio

Library of Congress Catalog Card Number 95-83622

ISBN 1-880687-10-0

Contents

Preface

Perhaps the most wonderful feeling that we can experience as human beings is that of love. Everything around us appears beautiful and radiant when we have this feeling. Good thoughts flow out to those around us, whatever we do turns out well, and the world is a great place to be.

But what is this feeling called love? Usually we associate it with something outside ourselves. We love some object or person, and because it makes us feel good we come to believe that it is the cause of our happiness. We search for objects that will please us, but even after attaining whatever we desire, we find that we are still not satisfied. Through reflection we realize that the feeling of peace and contentment actually comes from within ourselves. In fact, total happiness exists permanently within our own heart. Then why do we not experience this feeling at all times? This is the question which spirituality endeavors to answer by leading us to an understanding and experience of true love, the theme explored in this book.

All scriptures and sages proclaim that the Path of Love is the easiest of spiritual paths, as we all naturally have this affinity to love. In Part One, "Awakening to Love," we learn about the nature of love and how it relates to our everyday lives. Swami Abhedananda, a disciple of Sri Ramakrishna and spiritual brother of Swami Vivekananda, introduces the topic by declaring that love is the one power which governs our lives—a power inseparable from our own being. He says that all human affections are but manifestations of that wonderful power of love and goes on to describe the different types of love, those selfish and unselfish, temporary and permanent. He shows us how to spiritualize human affection in order to transform it into an expression of divine love in our daily life. The Buddhist writer Jack Kornfield explains that love, compassion, and equanimity involve being in the world and seeing the unity in things. He talks about the balance between active service in the world and meditation, and teaches us that love involves a fearlessness to give ourselves up to the unity. In this way we can come to see the truth of each moment.

The Vedantic Master Swami Chinmayananda points out how everything we need for our existence is given to us as a gift. In order to go beyond our slavery of indebtedness to the Giver of these gifts, the Lord, and turn the tables to become His master, we should offer everything we do, with true faith and devotion, as our gifts to Him. We do this by practicing such virtues as love and forgiveness. He demonstrates how the world outside reflects our own inner lives and thus provides evidence to the statement that we can only change the world by changing ourselves. Swami Tyagananda, editor of *Vedanta Kesari*, the Ramakrishna Vedanta Society's monthly journal, continues this line of thinking by showing us the role that gratitude to Nature, other people, and the Lord, in the form of love and service, plays in our spiritual development. The well-known American writer and teacher Leo Buscaglia writes on the importance of being able to love oneself in order to truly love and accept others. He encourages us to value our uniqueness and develop to our fullest potential in order to become the best, most loving beings we are capable of.

Part Two, "The Dynamics of Love," defines the components of true love as well as techniques by which we may develop this divine ability. John Powell, a Jesuit priest, begins this section detailing three important stages of love as kindness, encouragement, and challenge. In a pragmatic discussion he points out both the comforts and challenges of love in marriage and our relationships with others. Swami Chinmayananda states the fact that it is better to give than to receive love, and that through the act of giving one experiences true joy and complete self-fulfillment. He explains how we expand by giving love, and the importance of having no expectation to receive anything in return. He goes on to discuss the fundamental factors necessary for enduring love: a sincere concern for the beloved; a sense of deep response; an ardent attitude of reverence; and a complete understanding of the beloved. Eknath Easwaran, founder of the Blue Mountain Center of Meditation in Northern California, says that we cannot transform ourselves on the spiritual path without regular, systematic meditation. With this in mind, he gives an extensive commentary on the well-known prayer of St. Francis and shows us how we can use it as an instrument for effective meditation by turning our focus away from ourselves and reaching out to others. Vimala Thakar concludes this section pronouncing that by living in meditation, true compassion and love become realities which flow causelessly and abundantly when the defenses of the ego structure melt. She says that love is complete relaxation in wholeness, without any tension against oneself or others. It is being in easy communion with everything in life—its joys and sorrows, beauty and ugliness—without trying to manipulate others in any way; without trying to make them into something out of our own images.

Through these practices of meditation and sincere love—love in which others come first—we are led to the understanding of love in its highest form. Swami Amar Jyoti, head of the Truth Consciousness Society, begins Part Three, "Toward Divine Love," declaring that the highest love and the highest wisdom are one and the same. He distinguishes between relative and absolute love, saying that the latter is attained only after wisdom is born. What love ultimately means is the unity between you and your Lord—your Source. He says unconditional love is not seeking unity in uniformity, but rather, amid diversity. Only when the intellect and heart are united will we understand the relationship between the Absolute, God, and ourselves—that they are not three, but one. Next, Anthony de Mello, who was a Jesuit priest and director of an institute of pastoral counseling in Poona, India, says that we must drop our illusions and give up the drug of emotional dependence on others for the capacity of love to be born. To see with a vision unclouded by fear and desire is to love. The American writer Ralph Waldo Trine, a contemporary of Swami Abhedananda, tells us that God is the spirit of infinite love, and the more we love the closer we come to the realization of our oneness with that infinite love. We have all seen that a person with a positive attitude and a heart full of love attracts everyone to him or her. Part Three closes with an article by the inspirational writer Og Mandino, who gives us the secret of success through a number of practices based upon greeting each day with love in our heart.

Without love the spiritual path is barren and dry. Loving and understanding ourselves leads to the acceptance and love of all others. Constant discrimination and unselfish actions help us to perfect our love, and we come to experience our unity with all. Every action in life is motivated by the longing for this sense of completeness. Once we learn to love, we flow toward our true nature as naturally as a river flows toward the sea. Love truly conquers all!

L.S.

PART ONE

Awakening to Love

The lock of error shuts the gate,
open it with the key of love:
Thus, by opening the door,
thou shalt wake the Beloved.

Kabir

A finite subject cannot love, nor can a finite object be loved. When the object of the love of a man is dying every moment, and his mind also is constantly changing as he grows, what eternal love can you expect to find in this world? There cannot be any real love but in God; why then all these loves? These are mere stages. There is a power behind impelling us forward, we do not know where to seek for the real object, but this love is sending us forward in search of it. Again and again we find our mistake. We grasp something, and it slips through our fingers, and then we grasp something else. Thus on and on we go, till at last comes light; we come to God, the only One who loves. His love knows no change and is ever ready to take us in.

Swami Vivekananda

I

Human Affection and Divine Love

by Swami Abhedananda

The human soul possesses the germ of that indescribable something which poets, dramatists, artists, and philosophers of all ages have endeavored to describe by words and poems, by stories and fables, by symbols and images, by paintings and sculptures. That something is a charm which throws a spell around itself and whosoever comes near it remains enchanted and spellbound. It sweetens the bitter experiences of life, enlivens worried and dejected hearts and animates them with vigor, strength, hope, and cheerfulness. It makes one forget the drudgery of this world and infuses renewed energy to perform the duties of life and to enjoy the toils and troubles with peace, tranquility, and happiness. Were it not for that something, earthly existence would be dull and dreary, human hearts would be dry like a desert and expressions of human affection would be neither seen nor heard in this universe of transitory phenomena. The tie of friendship and the invisible cord that binds the hearts of parents and children, and unites the souls of a husband and a wife, or of a lover and the beloved, would be broken forever, if that something were not behind all these tender feelings and attachments which we call human affections. In fact, it is the unspeakable something which expresses itself as human love and human affection, brings peace and happiness to the soul, however momentary they may appear to be. Although it cannot be defined, still it has been called by various names in different countries. In the English language it is called *love*.

Whenever this word is uttered, it touches our hearts and creates a thrilling sensation in the soul of a genuine lover. All human affections are but the manifestations of that wonderful power of love. It is one power that governs our lives. It is inseparable from our being. We do not ask what is love, instinctively we understand its nature. Why?

Because from the very moment that we are conscious of our own existence we begin to love ourselves, either consciously or unconsciously. This love of self is to be found in lower animals as well as in human beings. Wherever there is the expression of self, there is also the manifestation of the love of self. Lower animals cannot know their love of self objectively, but they know it subjectively; they love themselves instinctively, unconsciously as it were. Man is the only animal which is capable of knowing his love of self objectively as well as subjectively.

In the lowest forms of animals this love of self is extremely limited in its sphere. It is confined to their bodies only. But when we rise a little higher in the animal kingdom we notice that in the species of Mammalia the love of self extends a little beyond their bodies. They feel for their offspring and take care of them as they do for their own bodies. This is the first expression of motherly affection. The same love gradually develops and manifests itself in man as human love, which is wider in range and stronger in power.

Animal love in man is the love of self which is identified with the gross physical body. The body being the center of love, animal love includes love of that which is connected with the body, of every object that is related to the physical form and of all things that bring a pleasing sensation or comfortable feeling to the animal self.

This love leads to the worship of the gross physical body. The vast majority of humanity love their bodies and bodily comforts. To them that is the be-all and end-all of life. They become strongly attached to their material forms and express their love of self by decorating their bodies with various things. From the tattooing of the body of a savage to the wearing of the most expensive garments and valuable jewels of a fashionable, up-to-date Parisian, at every step this love of self and worship of the body are manifested in different ways.

Animal love forces one to seek pleasures of the senses and physical comforts. This love of self as identified with the body is very narrow and limited. It is called attachment to the animal self, or selfishness. Animal love is blind and he who lives on this plane, is extremely selfish, cruel and heartless toward others; but when the same person rises above animal nature, his love becomes less selfish. He, then, feels for others as he feels for himself. It is then human love.

Every one of us living on the human plane is conscious of the feeling of human love, because all of mankind recognizes and loves a lover. Whenever and wherever a true lover appears, like a magnet he attracts and draws loving souls around him, and transforms them with the magnetic power of love. The loving heart of a true mother which sends forth the rays of motherly affection, awakens the germ of love that is latent in the soul of her child. Gradually it begins to respond, and becomes attached to its mother just as much as a true mother is attached to her little one. This strong feeling of attachment lies at the bottom of all human affection. As a loving mother is attached to her baby, so loving children, loving youths, and loving friends all become attached to one another. The difference is only in degree and not in kind. Mutual attachment and mutual dependence are the signs of human affection; and this strong attachment, again, is the result of a kind of attraction which exists in the nature of love.

The Nature of Love

The nature of love is to attract. Wherever there is an expression of love, there is manifested a kind of mutual attraction first, and then mutual attachment and mutual feeling of possession. But in the intensity of love that attachment becomes so close that the lover and the beloved both are united into one. They have two separate bodies; but their mind, heart, and soul are turned with the same key. When the one is struck, the other responds. Therefore we may say that the climax of attachment is reached when there is perfect union and absolute oneness between the lover and the beloved. The same attraction which is known on the material plane as gravitation, molecular attraction and chemical affinity, when manifesting itself on the soul plane, is called love.

Love is the attraction between a soul and a soul. Matter cannot attract the soul. Like attracts like. We may think by mistake that dead matter attracts the soul, but in reality it is the soul that attracts another soul. The mother loves the beautiful face of her child and kisses it. However ugly the child may be, the mother does not see that. We have never seen a mother who does not consider her newborn baby to be the best, finest, and most beautiful of all. Do you think that when a true mother loves the face of her child, she loves merely the material particles that make up its beautiful form? Certainly not. The particles of matter cannot attract the soul of the mother. It is the soul of the child lying behind the material face that attracts the soul of the mother. If the child dies, the same mother will not care for the material body of the dead baby. It is for this reason that Vedanta says: "A mother loves her child not for the child's sake, not for its material form, but for the sake of the soul, the *Ātman*, the Lord that lives in the child." The mother may not know it, but it is true, nevertheless. Similarly, "A wife loves her husband not for the sake of his physical form, but for the soul, the *Ātman* that lies behind his body." Whenever there is true love there is that pure attraction between two souls.

But ordinary human love or human affection which binds the soul to earthly conditions and makes it attached to the pleasures of the senses, and which is governed by selfish motives and selfish desires, is blind. It brings sorrow, suffering, and misery in the end. The excess of ordinary human affection generally leads to tragic results which we so often notice around us, and the graphic descriptions of which we so often read in the pages of the novels and dramas of the world.

Directing Love

Human affection, when governed by selfishness, produces a strong passion which rouses an animal craving for the gratification of the sense desires. From the standpoint of the world it is the most natural and most desirable thing, but from the standpoint of divine love it is nothing but misdirected love. It is an animal passion. All evil and wickedness which we find in a community and whatever is bad and sinful in a society is but the ill-directed working out of the feeling of love. It is the manifestation of selfish love, while all goodness and virtue are the results of acts which proceed from properly directed unselfish love.

Human affection, which lies at the root of murder, theft, robbery, and all sorts of vices, is extremely selfish. Human love when misdirected makes me a thief or a liar, a robber or a murderer, but when guided by unselfishness, leads to self-sacrifice, for the sake of another. A man who sacrifices his own life in saving that of another, loves another's life exactly in the same degree as a murderer loves his own self when he kills a man to enrich himself or to fulfill his selfish motive. The direction of love is proper and right in the case of the former, while in the case of the latter, it is improper and wrong.

Human affection naturally seeks a return of love. No one has ever seen a lover on the human plane in worldly life who does not expect to be loved in turn or who does not seek some kind of return for his or her love. But on the spiritual plane there are hundreds of instances where men and women have sacrificed everything, even their lives, for the love of some ideal, whether it is personal or impersonal, without seeking any return whatsoever. There is the expression of divine love. As long as love is mutual, that is, for the benefit of both the lover and the beloved, it is human. But when the stream of love flows toward an object simply for the good of the object and makes the lover forget himself for the time being, that love is uplifting and divine. Any thing or any act that makes us forget our small personality, our little individuality, our dear little self, is divine, because it leads Godward. That we should practice, that we should cultivate, and anything that emphasizes our small personality, that centers our thought upon the sense of *I, me, mine*—my opinion, my this and my that—is low down on the human plane, is not spiritual, is not divine. Human love or human affection which is limited by personality and is confined within the narrow sphere of personal self, and which strongly brings out the sense of *I, me, mine*, should be transformed into divine love by not thinking of one's self, by not seeking one's own comfort and pleasure, but by directing it toward the soul or the *Atman* of the beloved or toward the spiritual Ideal, which is divine and perfect.

Understanding the Eternal Ideal

It is true that human nature seeks companionship and longs for a suitable match for love; but all mortal companions on this plane are only for the time being. That craving of the soul will not be absolutely satisfied until the eternal object of love is discovered. The eternal object of love can be realized in the finite and concrete man or woman when we rise above the physical plane and understand that each individual soul is divine and immortal. It is a mere self-delusion to seek the fullness of love in any man or woman. Therefore, it is necessary to make the eternal Ideal the object of all human affection.

Father's love should recognize that ideal as his child. Mother's love should see it in her newborn baby; the love of a brother or of a sister should establish fraternal relation with It. A husband who is devoted to his wife should think of his eternal Ideal in the soul of his wife; and a wife should put her highest spiritual Ideal in the soul of her beloved husband and love him with her whole heart and soul. The love of a friend should look upon It as his dearest friend and the divine companion. In this way all earthly relations could be spiritualized and all human affection could in course of time be transformed into the expressions of divine love in daily life. There would be no more cause of dissatisfaction in a household, no more fighting between brothers and sisters, no more quarreling between parents and children, no more divorce on account of incompatibility of temper. Then each of these human affections will be like a path that leads to divine reality and eternal happiness. Each human affection will then find its right mark to the eternal father, divine mother, divine child, divine husband, and divine friend, since Vedanta teaches that divinity dwells in each individual soul and can be realized through any of these relations.

Personification of the Ideal

In India a true and sincere seeker after divine love personifies his divine Ideal in the form of an incarnation of God whom he worships as his divine master, and loves Him with his whole heart and soul, establishing all relations which are needed in human affection. He says: "O Lord, Thou art my mother, father, friend and relative; Thou art my knowledge and wealth; Thou art my all in all." A true lover of God thus forgets all earthly relations and enters into the holy spiritual family of his divine master. This is the spiritual birth of the soul. If absolute sincerity and earnestness be at the bottom of his heart, and if his love be truly unselfish, then the disciple through this devotion will eventually reach the supreme goal of divine love. The stream of human affection breaking down all the barriers of blood relation and the mountain of selfishness, falls in that river of divine love which is constantly flowing from the pure heart and unselfish soul of his spiritual master, into the infinite ocean of Divinity. Thus, the true disciple and the divine master become one in spirit and reach the goal together. In this sense a true spiritual master or divine incarnation may be called the mediator, the savior of such individual souls who are earnest and sincere seekers after spirituality and divine love. This is the path of love for those who are fortunate enough to find such an all-absorbing spiritual ideal or divine incarnation in a human form. Blessed are they who have become the disciples of a divine master.

In each individual heart is flowing a stream of love, which like a confined river constantly seeks an outlet through which it can run into that ocean of divine love which is called God. It may not find any outlet for many years or it may remain bottled up for ages within the narrow limits of animal self, but it never loses that innate tendency to run toward the infinite ocean of love. It must find its way out of that limitation sooner or later. Every drop of that stream of love which flows in a human heart, however, contains the germ of divine love. As a drop of water in a river contains all the chemical properties of the water of the ocean, so a drop of love, whether pure or impure, is of the same nature as a drop from the ocean of divine love. It varies in its character according to the direction toward which it flows and to the nature by which it is governed. When it flows toward one's own self it is animal; when toward another for mutual benefit or for earthly return, it is worldly and human; but when it is directed toward the divine Ideal it is divine.

Divine love brings a cessation of all sorrow, suffering and pain; it lifts the soul above all bondage, breaks the fetters of selfish attachment and worldliness. All selfishness vanishes and the soul enters into the abode of absolute freedom and everlasting happiness. The object of attachment in human affection is a changeable and mortal object, while the object of attachment in divine love is the unchangeable and immortal Being, the Lord of the universe.

Practicing Human Love and Affection

Some people have an erroneous notion that Vedanta teaches that we should not encourage human affection and human love. On the contrary, Vedanta teaches that our life on the human plane will be bitter and dry like a desert if it be not sweetened by human love. If the dewdrops of human affection do not moisten the dry and barren heart of a selfish man, how can the germ of divine love which is latent in each soul, sprout and grow into a big tree bearing the blossoms of kindness, sympathy, fellow compassion and all other tender feelings which produce the fruits of peace, freedom, and happiness! As long as we are on the human plane we should cultivate and practise human love and human affection. But when the soul learns by bitter experience that the object of human love and affection is only an ordinary mortal, when it longs for an immortal something which is higher and greater, when the soul rises from the human to the spiritual plane, and obtains glimpses of that which is unchangeable and absolute, how can such a soul be satisfied with human limitations and human imperfections! It is then that the soul longs for the expression of all affection on the spiritual plane. It is then that the soul becomes a seeker after the Absolute and a lover of the divine Ideal. Until that time has arrived one does not care for anything that is higher than human affection. As on the human plane, forced love is never sweet and genuine, so on the spiritual plane love for the spiritual ideal or divine master must be spontaneous and intense, unwavering and whole-souled; otherwise dissatisfaction and unhappiness will be the result, if it be forced in any way by any being. Therefore, according to Vedanta human affection and divine love each has its value in its own sphere.

Divine love seeks no return. Whenever there is a feeling of getting anything as a return of love, it is like a shopkeeper's love for his customer, or like a paid servant's love for his master. There is no expression of unselfish love in the service of a paid servant, because he is bound to serve, otherwise he will not receive his wage, and will be dismissed. True love does not manifest itself in bondage or slavery, but in freedom. Similarly, a person who serves God for some kind of return has no unselfish love in his heart. A priest who receives a salary for his service or preaching, does not serve, does not preach through pure love, but for that return. If he did not get his recompense he would stop preaching. But he works through pure love whose work is a free offering to the world. Such a person never thinks of earning his livelihood by selling his works. He is sure that the world would feed him and take care of him. He never thinks of the morrow, but the morrow thinks of him. This grand expression of divine love was demonstrated in the lives of Jesus Christ, Buddha, Chaitanya, Ramakrishna, and other great preachers of Truth. The commercial instinct of many of the modern preachers has blinded their eyes with a veil of worldliness and shopkeeper's love, and therefore they do not see the true spirit of Christ's teachings. How many religious teachers of today explain that divine love which knows no return, and how few preachers do preach without seeking any remuneration for their labor? There is a great difference between a professional preacher and a true lover of God. The one is a beggar, a shopkeeper, and the other offers freely what he has to give and thinks of no return of wealth, name, fame, or social position.

The Fruits of Divine Love

Divine love brings nonattachment to worldly pleasures and removes all fear of punishment. Can there be love in a slave who serves his master through fear of being punished if he did not serve? Can there be love in the heart of a devotee who worships

God to avoid eternal punishment? No. Love and fear cannot dwell in the same place at the same time. Fear proceeds from attachment to self, while true love makes one unattached to self. Fear and love are like two opposite poles. Divine love conquers all fear. Do we not see that when a girl truly falls in love with her lover she loses all fear? She is not afraid of her parents, relatives, the criticism of her friends, the social customs, the laws of the state, not even death. So a true lover of God does not fear anything in the universe. With this intense feeling of fearlessness the martyrs have boldly faced brutal persecution, excruciating agony and have gone to the stake to be burned alive with a smiling countenance.

A true lover of God loves everything of the world. He does not see good or evil, misery or sorrow, disease or death. Divine love opens his spiritual eye and he realizes that everything comes from God, that everything is God's, that all living creatures are His children. He sees the divine ideal as manifesting Himself through all animate and inanimate objects of the universe. So he cannot help loving everything and all creatures equally. He feels that nothing in the world can happen without God's will. He surrenders his individual will to the universal Will. Resigning himself entirely to the all knowing Will, he welcomes most heartily everything good or bad that comes in his way. If a disease comes, he says, "My Beloved has sent me His guest. I must take care of him, and serve him." He thinks himself extremely blessed at every moment of his life, and welcomes death as he would welcome his most beloved sister, saying: "Come sister Death, come and take the offering of my body." How can such a soul be afraid of death? This type of a true lover of God is still to be found in India. Absolute self-surrender and self-resignation take away all fear. This is the state when a man can say from the very bottom of his soul and with perfect assurance: "Let Thy Will be done, and not mine." Ordinary persons repeat it like a parrot without having any feeling of true self-surrender in their hearts.

Divine love brings nonattachment to worldly pleasures and enjoyments. A true mother forgets all pleasures and enjoyments when she kisses and fondles her newborn baby; that all-absorbing motherly love swallows up her attachment to other things and makes her extremely attached to the child; she unconsciously renounces every other thought. So a true lover of God unconsciously renounces the desires for any other pleasure or enjoyment. Therefore, divine love makes him unattached to the things of the world. It brings to the soul absolute freedom from the bondage of selfishness and ignorance.

It is nobler and better than good works, greater than knowledge, higher than concentration and meditation, because all these end in divine love, while divine love is its own end. It is the easiest path of all. Divine love straightens out all crookedness of the heart and destroys the germs of vanity and self-conceit which are deeply rooted in the human soul. It cannot be confined by any scripture, but the words and deeds of such a true lover of God become the scriptures of the world. Divine love brings the highest ecstatic or superconscious state in which the individual soul eternally communes with God, the universal Spirit. It this state of ecstasy the soul of a *bhakta* becomes intoxicated, as it were, with the wine of divine love. He cannot stand on his feet, he talks in a tongue which no one can understand. Ordinary persons may call him insane because they do not know him in the least.

In India I saw Bhagavan Sri Ramakrishna who is regarded as the latest divine manifestation of the present age. He attained to this ecstasy and lived as the perfect embodiment of divine love. In his ecstatic condition he used to be intoxicated just as much as a drunkard would be after drinking bottles of wine. Many people imagined that perhaps he was in the habit of drinking; and when he used to talk in a tongue unknown to human beings they thought that he was mad. Hearing these remarks Ramakrishna replied: "Yes, what people say is perfectly true. In the insane asylum of this world who is not mad? Everyone is mad after something or other; one is mad after a wife, another after a husband, a third after wealth, some after name, fame or objects of ambition or power. Show me one who is not made after any one of these transitory things, but I am mad after God, who is eternal and everlasting, the Soul of my soul; which is better?"

II

Spiritual Practice and Social Action

by Jack Kornfield

How can we reconcile the question of service and responsibility in the world with the Buddhist concepts of nonattachment, emptiness of self, and nonself? First we must learn to distinguish love, compassion, and equanimity from what might be called their "near-enemies."

The near-enemy of love is attachment. It masquerades as love: "I love this person, I love this thing," which usually means, "I want to hold it, I want to keep it, I don't want to let it be." This is not love at all; it is attachment, and they are different. There is a big difference between love, which allows and honors and appreciates, and attachment, which grasps and holds and aims to possess.

The near-enemy of compassion is pity. Instead of feeling the openness of compassion, pity says, "Oh, that poor person! They're suffering; they're different from me," and this sets up separation and duality. "That is outside me. I want it. I need it to be complete." I and it are seen as different.

The near-enemy of equanimity is indifference. It feels very equanimous to say, "I don't give a damn, I don't care, I'm not really attached to it," and in a way it is a very peaceful feeling, a great relief. Why is that? Because it is a withdrawal. It is a removal from the world and from life. Can you see the difference?

Equanimity, like love and compassion, is not a removal. It is being in the middle of the world and opening to it with balance, seeing the unity in things. Compassion is a sense of our shared suffering. Equanimity is a balanced engagement with life. The "near-enemies"—attachment, pity, and indifference—all are ways of backing away or removing ourselves from the things which cause fear. Meditation does not lead to a departure from the world. It leads to a deeper vision of it, one which is not self-centered, which moves from a dualistic way of viewing (I and other) to a more spontaneous, whole, unified way.

Vimala Thakar has been a meditation teacher in India and Europe for many years. In many ways, she is a Dharma heir to Krishnamurti. After she had been working in rural development for many years, Krishnamurti asked her to begin to teach, and she became a powerful and much-loved meditation teacher. Then she returned to her rural development work, teaching meditation considerably less. I asked her, "Why did you go back to rural development and helping the hungry and homeless after teaching meditation?" and she was insulted by my question. She said, "Sir"—as Krishnamurti does—"I am a lover of life, sir, and I make no distinction between serving people who are starving and have no dignity in their physical lives and serving people who are fearful and closed and have no dignity in their mental lives. There is no difference to me. I love all of life, and the way that I give is to respond to whatever is presented to me."

It was a wonderful response! There is a Sufi or Islamic phrase that puts it together. It says, "Praise Allah, and tie your camel to the post." It expresses both sides: pray, yes, but also make sure you do what is necessary in the world. It is what Don Juan called "a balance between controlled folly and impeccability." Controlled folly means seeing that all of life is a show of light and sound and that this tiny blue-green planet hangs in space with millions and billions of stars and galaxies, and that people have only been here for one second of world time compared with millions of years of other changes. This context helps us to laugh more often, to enter into life with joy. The quality of impeccability entails realizing how precious life is, even though it is transient and ephemeral, and how, in fact, each of our actions and words do count, each affects all the beings around us in a very profound way.

Uniting Meditation and Service

If I wanted, I could make a very convincing case for just practising sitting meditation and doing nothing else; and an equally convincing case for going out and serving the world. Looking at it from the first side, does the world need more oil and energy and food? Actually, no. There are enough resources for all of us. There is starvation, poverty, and disease because of ignorance, prejudice, and fear, because we hoard and create wars over imaginary geographic boundaries and act as if one group of people is different from another. What the world needs is not more oil, but more love and generosity, kindness and understanding. Until those are attained, the other levels will never work. So you really have to sit and meditate and get that understanding in yourself first. Only when you have actually done it yourself can you have the insight to effectively help change the greed in the world and to love. Thus, it is not a privilege to meditate, but a responsibility. I will not go any further with this argument, but it is very convincing.

As for the other side, I only have to mention Cambodia or Somalia and the starvation in Central Africa and India, where the enormity of the suffering is beyond comprehension. In India alone, 350 million people live in such poverty that they have to work that day to get enough food to feed themselves that night, when they are lucky. I once interviewed a man in Calcutta who was 64 years old and pulled a rickshaw for a living. He had been pulling it for 40 years, and he had ten people dependent on him for income. He had gotten sick once the year before for ten days, and after a week they ran out of money and had nothing to eat.

How can we let this happen? Forty deaths per minute from star-vation in the world; $714,000 a minute spent on machines to kill people. We must do something!

Both arguments are totally convincing. The question is how to choose what to do, what path to take, where to put our life energy, even which spiritual path to follow. Spirituality in this country has blossomed and it is exquisite! It is also kind of con-fusing. There are so many ways to go, how to decide? How can we choose what to do this year, today? For me the answer has been to simply follow the heart. Sometimes it is clear that we must take time to meditate and simplify—to do our inner work. Sometimes it is clear that we must begin to act and give and serve.

I can just share my own experience, which is very immedi-ate. Ordinarily I spend my year teaching meditation retreats. A couple of years ago, though, war began raging in Cambodia. I know the people there and a couple of the local languages, and something in me said, "I am going," and I went, not for very long but long enough to be of some assistance. This year, feeling a real need to bring a greater marriage of service and formal medi-tation, I went to India again with some friends to collect tapes for radio and television on the relationship between spiritual practice and social responsibility. And now I am back teaching meditation.

I did not think about it much at the time. It just seemed that it had to be done, and I went and did it. It was something imme-diate and personal. The spiritual path does not hold out some simple solution, some easy formula for everyone to follow. It is not a question of imitation. You cannot be like Mother Teresa. She is Mother Teresa, and she is wonderful. Even if you tried, you wouldn't be like her. You have to be yourself. That means listening to your heart and knowing the right thing to do, and then doing it in the spirit of growing in awareness and service.

It is not always easy. Nobody said it was supposed to be. It is not even easy getting out of the womb. There is a lot that is hard in having a human birth. It is difficult, but it is also beautiful. There is a story about Mother Teresa and her ring. Someone said to Mother Teresa, "Well, you know, it is easier for you. You are not married or in a relationship."

"What do you mean? I am married," she answered, holding up the ring that signifies a nun's marriage to Jesus, "and He can be very difficult, too!"

The Force of Fearlessness

There are two great forces in this world. One is the force of killing. That is how dictators run countries. They run them by killing other people—by being willing and not being afraid to kill. But there is another great force that is equally powerful, maybe more so, and that is the force of not being afraid to die. That is the only force that is powerful enough to meet someone who is not afraid to kill. What Gandhi showed in India was the power of this force. Thousands of troops came from one direction to partition and to quell the riots, while from the other direction came one person, Gandhi, whose strategy eventually succeeded. How did he do it? He said, "I am going to starve. I won't eat until you stop the rioting and insanity." He knew that his people cared so much for him, they would not let him die. That is what love is—putting yourself on the line. The spirit of service, in little ways and big ways, is really what practice is: serving ourselves, serving the world around us. It is a giving of ourselves or a giving up of ourselves to the unity, the whole, and not just this little "I-me-mine." It is powerful and joyful, really wonderful to learn to give.

One of the exquisite experiences in my travels in India was to see the holy city of Benares on the Ganges River bank, covered with hundreds of temples and stores and markets. Along the Ganges there are bathing ghats, where people come to pay their respects and bathe as a purification, and there are also ghats where they bring bodies to burn. I had heard about them for years and had always thought, "Wow, that must be a heavy place. They bring bodies there and they burn them and it must be really intense." It was amazing to be rowed in this little boat down the Ganges in a very quiet way up to where there were twelve different fires going, and six or eight of them had bodies on them. Every half an hour or so, they would carry a new body down to the fires, chanting, "*Rama Nama Satya Hei*," which could be translated as "The only truth is the name of God." Yet it was not heavy at all. It was peaceful and quiet and sane. It was really sane. It was just, "Well, that is what happens."

Opening Our Hearts

What does this have to do with meditation practice? It has to do with the recognition that, in the face of the tremendous suffering of the world, there can be joy that comes not from denying pain and seeking pleasure, but from our ability to sit in meditation, even when it is difficult, and to let our hearts open to our experience. It is really the nitty-gritty work of practice to sit here and feel your sadness and my sadness and our fear, our desperation and our restlessness, to open to them and begin to learn that to love is to die to how we wanted it to be, and to open more to its truth. To love is to accept. It is not a weakness. It is the most extraordinary power.

There is a beautiful sutra that talks about the blessings of those who grow in this kind of love. It is called the Cultivation of Lovingkindness, and it lists 50 blessings that come through diligent practice. It says that if your heart is open and loving, you will have sweet dreams and fall asleep more easily, and awaken contented, with a smile. The devas and angels will love and protect you. Men and women will love you, and weapons will not be able to harm you. Guns will misfire, and poison won't work, and things that come to harm you will not be able to, it is such a powerful force. People will welcome you everywhere into their countries and into their homes, and you will have pleasant thoughts, and your mind will become very quiet. Animals will sense this love, and they will love you back. Elephants will bow to you. Your voice will become sweet and soft, and your babies will be happy in the womb and happy when they grow up. If you fall off a cliff, it says, a tree will always be there to catch you. Your countenance will be serene, your eyes shiny, and you will become awakened.

Even though this is what the sutra says will happen, we don't talk about lovingkindness early on in our retreats. People are sitting with restlessness and anger and knee pains, not joy, peace, or serenity. But I will tell you a secret, what is really important in the practice: true love is really the same as awareness. They are identical. Not the near-enemies of "I want" or "I am in love with" but deeper love than that. True love is to see the divine goodness, the Buddha nature, the truth of each moment, and to say, "Yes," to allow ourselves to open, to accept. That is our practice every moment, whether in sitting meditation or action-meditation, whether sitting on a cushion or sitting near the barricades in protest. It is to be aware, to see the truth which frees us. It is opening to what is now, to what is here, and to seeing it as it is.

The forces of injustice in the world loom so huge, and sometimes we feel so tiny. How are we to have an impact? I will leave you with the words of Don Jose in Castaneda's *Tales of Power*: "Only if one loves this earth with unbending passion can one release one's sadness. A warrior is always joyful because his love is unalterable and his beloved, the earth, bestows upon him inconceivable gifts. . . . Only the love for this splendorous being can give freedom to a warrior's spirit; and freedom is joy, efficiency, and abandon in the face of any odds."

III

Returning
the Gift

by Swami Chinmayananda

If the world was not there, we could not survive upon the surface of the globe for even a moment. When I say the world, it includes everything: the sun, moon, stars, the plant and animal kingdoms, the earth itself, and the rivers and oceans. The entire world is necessary for us to exist. This is why in the scriptural narration of creation all religions declare that the world was created first and then man was introduced, and not the other way around. Christianity relates the story of how Adam was formed in the Garden of Eden. In ancient Hinduism also the world was created first and the last masterpiece of creation was man. The Lord was so happy in making His masterpiece that He sent him to the world with certain instructions. "You do not need to approach the Lord to improve the world-condition, but you are the master of the entire universe."

These are not just stories; it is true. The world is necessary for our existence. To that extent we are all slaves to the world. If the sun, moon, and stars were not there; if the gravitational or phenomenal forces, the air in the atmosphere, or water were not there we could not exist. All of nature is necessary for us to survive and enjoy life.

Everything that exists, this entire world is given to us as a gift from the creator, the Lord. Are the sun, moon, stars, and the oxygen not free? If these are not there, of what use is our technology? Not only the outer world, but the equipment to contact that world—our eyes, ears, nose, tongue, mind and intellect—are also gifts. Yet in our vanity we think that we are achieving certain things, but we could not achieve anything if it were not for all these gifts. Therefore, our achievements are also ultimately only gifts. When we start thinking deeply about these ideas, the logic of it becomes self-evident.

When a gift is received, the recipient is a slave and the giver is the master. We, the entire humanity, are slaves, recipients, in the sense that the Lord is the giver, the Master. An employee who receives a monthly salary from her employer is a recipient, and in spite of what the labor law says, is a slave to her employer.

The True Meaning of Spirituality

The great thinkers of the past, the rishis, were allergic to the idea of slavishness. They did not want to be slaves to anyone, not even to God. Their entire system revolted against the idea that they would only be recipients, beggars at His door at every moment. So these great revolutionaries started thinking, is it possible that even though He is the omnipotent, omnipresent, omniscient Lord of the entire universe, I can still become the Master? And their great discovery to humanity was that we can conquer Him, and He can be our implicit slave. The method of achieving this is the meaning of spirituality.

Whatever we have been giving is His gift to us. How can we give Him anything when nothing is mine? The great rishis pondered over this question and found out a strategy by which the Lord can be walking behind us, wagging His tail as an implicit slave. How is this possible? It is true that whatever we have is His gift to us, but what we do with what we have is our gift to Him. When we start giving Him the gift, He becomes the recipient. When He becomes the recipient, He is a slave and we are the Master.

Let me give an example. Suppose there is a servant who has been faithfully working for your family for the last twenty years. Today he will be the head of the family, although he is still paid by you and working in the kitchen, yet everybody surrenders to him implicitly. How did this happen? It is because of the way he worked for you with all loyalty and honesty, taking even better care of your health than you would yourself, that you now do whatever he says. Once this is understood, we should learn to apply all our faculties—physical, mental, and intellectual—in His service. All scriptures advise us to have the attitude, "Thy will be done, not mine, not mine. I am only an instrument, Oh Lord, make use of me."

In Advaita philosophy, this omnipotent, omnipresent *Brahman* is the cause for the universe. Cause is never away from the effect. All the effects are nothing but the cause in different forms. All waves are nothing but the ocean in different forms. The entire universe around us has come from Him, the cause. That cause is unachieved, ever pursued, pervading in all beings. Therefore, if all my faculties are made use of or employed for the benefit of others and not for my own selfish desires, am I not offering Him the very faculties that He has given to me?

No doubt, I am a limited creature, and cannot be omnipresent, but He is present everywhere—in every plant, animal, and human being. I can serve Him anywhere as every name and form is nothing but His moving temple, a touch of life. This vitality that vibrates through every living being is the Self, the Lord.

Thus, when I start serving everybody, without consideration of caste, creed, color, belief or behavior, whether he is a cruel monster or a divine individual, I am serving nothing but the Lord. So when we surrender our stupid egos, our vulgar selfishness, and start using all our faculties for the service of others, we know that He is the one who receives through all these names and forms.

Try this method for six months and then just look back. You will find the Lord standing there, ready to do whatever you want

Him to do. He has to, because He has become the recipient. He is an employee, and I am now the employer. I am giving to Him and He has to accept. He has no choice. We cannot deny His gift because it is thrust upon us. Similarly, when we fling our works upon Him, the poor Lord will have to be our slave. The Lord is always a slave to his devotees. When I use the word "devotee" do not think of one who goes on pilgrimages every year and gives money and gold to the temple. That is not devotion. Devotion means devotion to the Lord at every moment. This kind of devotion is now sadly lost in the world.

Faith and Devotion

With the arrival of the scientific revolution, the West said farewell to devotion and faith. No doubt, a lot has been achieved, but the loss of faith and devotion has caused many harmful results. We have achieved significant conquests over nature, but the callous aspects of our nature within have rapidly gained possession over us. In thoughts, ideas, and actions, some people have become worse than animals. This is what is now called technological development!

The virtues of compassion, mercy, tenderness, love, and forgiveness, which add to the glory of humanity, have all but disappeared. All over the world, the entire order of things has become disturbed. Years ago it was discovered that tampering with nature leads to disastrous results, and out of this came a new science called ecology. If damage to nature continues in this way, man will disappear from the surface of the globe.

The purely material outlook and values that have replaced devotion and faith in man—that have made him selfish in the extreme, that have propogated the philosophy that only the fittest can survive—have caused a maladjusted economy all over the world, where the rich continue to grow richer and the poor helplessly become poorer. Markets slump while the poor find prices of goods increasingly beyond their means.

We are desperately in need of tranquility and peace to alleviate the hardships of vast populations living in appalling conditions all over the world. But instead we have undeclared wars going on in many parts of the world—in South Africa, South America, Middle East, North Africa, Afghanistan, Iraq, Iran, and Kampuchea—which are directly or indirectly supported by certain big powers. Not to mention the ecological imbalances, the depletion of the ozone layer that causes untimely rains, failure of monsoons, and unseasonable snowfalls upsetting the natural rhythm of life.

Nature Only Reflects

Nature only reflects humanity, however. An echo is dependent on the sound we make. When we are in a valley and we cry out "you are a fool," the valley echoes back "you are a fool" three times. If we hate the world, we receive hatred back threefold. If, on the other hand, we learn to love the world, we will receive triple that love. We ourselves are the deciding factors. If we act poorly, nature will behave poorly. If we act wisely, nature changes immediately and will be beneficial and benevolent to us. In the third chapter of the *Bhagavad Gita*, Lord Krishna says that the creators order that when we are cherished by the yagna spirit, by society or the community, we shall cherish them back. Thus mutually, man cherishing nature, and nature cherishing man, we may reach the highest prosperity, peace, and joy.

Until we change, the world is not going to change. To the modern world of politics or sociology, the world outside, called nature, is something to be manipulated. Just as though it is a machine that can be corrected and repaired. But it is not an inanimate thing. The outer world is a living, pulsating organism. The great thinkers of India recognized that it is His form, the infinite Reality. It is not a thing to be manipulated, but something to be cultivated and nourished, respected, and revered. If nature is approached with the right attitude we can get things done by invoking His grace and blessings.

We may say, "But what is the use, I am just a nobody. How can I make a difference?" But any one of us can conquer and direct the universe around us because we are the center. The best definition of infinity is, "The infinite is a circle whose circumference is nowhere and whose center is everywhere." Meaning, every one of us is a center of the entire universe. When we change, the world will change. We may wonder why our country is the way it is, but we ourselves are the cause. Why? Because we have not purified ourselves.

If I am an alcoholic right now, only alcoholics will come around me, and I say that they are the cause for my drinking. But if I decide to stop drinking only teetotalers will come around me. Now how did I change the world around me? I changed the world by changing myself.

When we feel that nobody loves or respects us what should we do? Begin to respect everyone, love everyone with a full heart, and they will in turn love and respect us. It cannot be any other way. Do not ask anyone's permission first! Splash it around. Love means love without any desire. Love with desire is called lust. Share pure love and anyone coming near us must feel that love. If we go near a fire we must feel hot, not cold. It cannot be otherwise; it is a universal law. Similarly, love generates love.

We have forgotten all these beautiful techniques of mastering the world around us, improving the country, beautifying our society, in short, transforming the world by changing ourselves. Without changing ourselves the world is not going to change. Revolutions or changes in the constitution will not change or bring peace to the world.

What we have been given is His gift to us, but what we do with what we have is our gift to Him. I give Him a gift by more intelligently putting to use what has been given to me. With my gift I conquer Him and make Him a slave. He will be there, behind me. Why? Because I am serving the entire world. If that attitude is taken by everyone, the improvement of the country will come about and the world will change by itself.

When we are healthy, our reflection in the mirror is healthy. When we are unhealthy, we may want to break all the mirrors because we do not like what we see, but the mirror is honest, it reflects exactly what is in front of it. So remember how others may be enjoying or suffering when they have to look at us.

When we develop our own health—physical, mental, and spiritual—our reflection, the world, will change. The outside world is a mirror to ourselves because the world outside is ruled and determined by the condition of our own inner world. Each of us is responsible for the condition of the world today. Therefore, let us try to change the world by changing ourselves.

IV

The Spirit of Gratitude

by Swami Tyagananda

Gratitude is not just a matter of a thank you or some form of visible acknowledgment of the help we have received. These are outer—and usually superficial—ways of expressing our gratitude. They may be OK and sometimes even obligatory as a form of social etiquette, but they need not necessarily indicate that we are really grateful. It is possible to say a warm thank you without being serious about it.

Obviously, *real* gratitude must proceed from the center of our personality. How is this *real* gratitude expressed? Through love and reverence. We love and revere not only the benefactor but also the benefit he or she has bestowed on us. We use those gifts in the best possible manner for ourselves as well as for others. Making the optimum use of our gifts is perhaps the best way to be grateful for the gifts received. When we use the gifts well, the message is loud and clear: "I care for your loving presentation. I am grateful to you."

If we look back at our lives we will be astonished to find what an enormous number of things there are we need to be grateful for. Let us begin with our parents, who were the first human beings we encountered as little babies. We could do nothing on our own then. We were fully dependent on them, particularly on our mothers. Have we cared to pause and ponder over their tireless, selfless labor, the continual sacrifices, and the unending care and love we received from them in those early years? They fed us, clothed us, nursed us back to health when we fell ill, and played with us. When we grew up a little, they arranged for our schooling and other facilities. In the years that followed they were our constant source of support, encouragement, love, and security. How do we express our gratitude for all these things? It might be argued that our parents did everything because that is what they are supposed to do, it was their *duty*. We may appreciate their conscientiousness, but there is no question of being grateful for it. Now, that is an interesting point and it brings in a host of other related matters.

A group of Sikhs used to visit Sri Ramakrishna at Dakshineswar. They said to him once, "God is compassionate." Sri Ramakrishna smiled and asked them, "To whom is He compassionate?" "To all of us," they said. "But we are His children," Sri Ramakrishna told them. "Does compassion to one's own children mean much? A father must look after his children; or do you expect the people of the neighborhood to bring them up?" Let us apply this insight to our earthly father and mother. We shall return to our Heavenly Father and Mother a little later.

So then, our parents did their duty in bringing us up, and to that extent there seems little meaning in thanking them for it. This may be a little difficult to understand for those in the West, for there one says thank you all the time for every little thing. Their prayers to God are also profusely filled with expressions of gratitude. A day called "Thanksgiving" is set apart every year when believers offer special thanks to God for all the bounties He has bestowed on them. But the Eastern tradition is different. In India no thanks are offered to God. No one says thank you to one's parents, teachers, children, and friends. Verbal thanking is considered a very formal gesture, tolerable in official dealings and among strangers, but not expected, even discouraged, in almost all other situations. Once Sister Nivedita, by force of habit, said thank you to a young Indian who had brought her a glass of water. She was quick to notice the subtle expression of pain on the young man's face, hurt as he was that the love and reverence with which he had done the little service to her was, so to say, compensated and neutralized by the two words: Thank You. She was careful from then on not to let this Western habit encroach on her dealings with those belonging to her adopted country.

Expressions of Gratitude

But not saying thank you is not the same thing as not being grateful. If our parents did *their* duty by looking after and caring for us, we must do *our* duty by being grateful for all that they have done. A million thank you's cannot compensate for even a tiny fraction of their sacrifice and love. Our gratitude to them, therefore, must show through our lives in the form of love and respect, obedience and service. When the Vedic rishi asked his students to look upon their parents as gods, he certainly had this idea of gratitude in mind. The guru is our spiritual parent; so gratitude to him too takes the form of love and respect, obedience and service. A faithful, vigorous and enthusiastic practice of the disciplines taught by the guru is one sure indication that the disciple is everlastingly grateful to him.

What about our secular teachers, our friends, our colleagues, and just everyone from whom we have received something or other? We must be grateful to all of them by utilizing in the best possible way whatever we have received. We must also be ready to give them or share with them whatever they are in need of. But it is best not to link up what we have received with what we give. If such connection somehow takes place, gratitude becomes just another name for sanctified shopkeeping, a very subtle form of give-and-take: "I do this for you because you did something for me some time ago." Though it may not be expressed in such a blunt manner, the idea of selfless service is completely absent in this transaction. True gratitude and "shop-keeping" cannot go together.

We must be grateful to Nature for the air we breathe, the water we drink, the food we eat, the land we live on. The mountains, the sun, the rain, the rivers. . . . Nature's treasures are infinite and she shares them with all, freely and ungrudgingly. Our gratitude to Nature should show through the responsible and positive use we make of natural resources. Nature has sufficient to meet all our needs, but not enough to quench our greed. Those who are engaged in a greedy, selfish exploitation of Nature's treasures are nothing less than ungrateful brutes. They are the cause of the environmental pollution on this fragile planet on which we live. The major threats to the earth's environment today come from the destruction of forests and other habitats; the global warming due to emissions of carbon dioxide and other greenhouse gases; the unending production of household garbage and toxic industrial waste which cannot be recycled; the release of chlorofluorocarbons into the atmosphere, resulting in the depletion of the ozone layer that protects living things from dangerous ultraviolet rays; and the chopping down of forests, overgrazing of grasslands, and overploughing of croplands in a desperate effort to feed the ever-increasing population. All these are sad reminders of the fact that humankind in general has lost the reverence for life and its handmaiden, Nature. When ingratitude and selfishness go hand in hand, there is cause for real alarm. A few voices of concern about the rape of the environment and Nature are being heard and positive steps to stem the tide are being taken in some parts of the world—but so far, at least, they have been fighting a losing battle.

Leading an Ideal Life

Our ingratitude to the Reality *beyond* Nature is equally appalling. Everything comes to us from God. We ourselves have come from Him. We owe Him our very existence. Our gratitude to Him should be the greatest. And how is this gratitude to be expressed? By leading an ideal life—the kind of life He wants us to lead. He has given every one of us a "mobile home"—the body. We must take good care of it, and use it for an all-round welfare, our own and others. He has given us speech—not to indulge in falsehood and slander, but to uphold truth and virtue. He has given every one of us a mind—not to make it a breeding ground for hatred, jealousy, envy, anger, lust, and greed, but to be a powerhouse of love, justice, selflessness, and self-control. The mind was given to us not to think vague, useless, or destructive thoughts, but to cultivate noble, elevating, and positive thoughts. God has given everyone of us an intellect—not to cheat our fellowmen or to invent weapons of mass-destruction, but to probe the mystery of life, internal and external, so that we may find our way to the freedom Absolute. Let every faculty God has given us be used to glorify God and His creation. One who does it well is a truly grateful child of God, not he who mumbles thanksgiving prayers five times a day but lives an ungodly life.

Time cannot be divided. All its so-called divisions are man-made, but they do serve some useful purpose. Take, for instance, the division of time into years, months, and days. The beginning of a year is a good time to review how grateful we have been so far. Let us look back at everything we have received from the world and ask ourselves whether we have made a proper use of all those things. Let us also turn our eyes inward and face the silence of the Eternal Presence within our hearts. "Have I made good use of all that came to me through the boundless mercy of God? Have I done anything—Oh! how *many* things!—to displease Him? Have I, His child, betrayed the faith He reposed in me when He sent me forth to study in this big school called the world? Have I been an ideal child of God? Have I been a good student of life?" Answers to these questions will determine how grateful we have been.

There is no need to despair if our past performance has

not exactly been what we wish it was. What has happened, has happened. Time cannot be rolled back like a carpet. Perhaps our past failures were necessary to prepare us for our future successes. If we take care not to repeat our past failures, success can be ours for the asking.

The question before us today must be: "If I continue to do what I am doing now, would I be a better person next year?" If some change in our life pattern is called for, let us make it at once. It is never too late, but, certainly, the earlier we wake up the better. Let us, if necessary, rearrange our lives, get our priorities straightened out, and wipe the dust off our minds to get a clearer vision of what lies ahead—so that when we begin to review our lives this time next year, we should be in a happier position than we are now in. This will, of course, depend on how we handle our lives in the course of *this* year. Success is not a destination, it is a journey. There is no end to being successful in life, secular or spiritual. Real success always depends on how much we have learned to be grateful. The spirit of gratitude and lasting success are inseparable.

V

Loving Oneself

by Leo Buscaglia

To love others you must love yourself. . . . You can only give to others what you have yourself. This is especially true of love. You cannot give what you have not learned and experienced. Since love is not a thing, it is not lost when given. You can offer your love completely to hundreds of people and still retain the same love you had originally. It is like knowledge. The wise man can teach all he knows and when he is through he will still know all that he has taught. But first he must have the knowledge. It would better be said that man "shares" love, as he "shares" knowledge, but he can only share what he possesses.

Loving oneself does not imply an ego-centered ability like the old witch in *Snow White* who reveled in the process of gazing into her mirror and asking, "Mirror, mirror on the wall, who is the fairest one of all." Loving oneself does mean a genuine interest, caring, concern and respect for oneself. To care about oneself is basic to love. Man loves himself when he sees himself with accuracy, genuinely appreciates what he sees, but is especially excited and challenged with the prospect of what he can become.

Discovering Our Uniqueness

Each person is unique. Nature abhors sameness. Each flower in the field is different, each blade of grass. Have you ever seen two roses alike, even among the same variety? No two faces are exactly alike, even in identical twins. Our fingerprints are singularly ours that we can be positively identified by them. But man is a strange creature. Diversity frightens him. Instead of accepting the challenge, the joy, the wonder of variation, he usually is frightened of it. He either moves away from or endeavors to twist uniqueness into sameness. Only then does he feel secure.

Each child born is an unmarked creation, a new combination of wonder. In general, his or her human anatomy is similar to others, but on a subtle level even how this anatomy functions will vary with each individual. His personality development seems to have common elements which affect it; heredity, environment, chance. But there is surely an additional element, not yet scientifically identifiable, which can be called the "X" factor of personality, that special combination of forces which act upon the individual so that he will react, respond, perceive as himself, alone. The child is exceptional but most learning which he will receive from birth will not afford him the freedom to discover and develop this uniqueness.

As we have indicated previously, the true function of a child's education should be the process of helping him to discover his uniqueness, aiding him toward its development, and teaching him how to share it with others. Rather, education is an "imposition" of what is called "reality" upon the child. Society, on the other hand, should be the agent through which his uniqueness is shared, for it is in dire need of fresh, new approaches to individual and group living. But society has the idea that what has been for centuries, even if it has not proven true, is the best way. This fallacy, if adhered to, leads individuality to its doom.

Each child offers a new hope for the world. But this thought apparently frightens most people. What would society be like made up of all "individuals?" Would it not be unruly and lead to anarchy? We recoil in horror at this thought. We feel more comfortable with a "silent majority." We distrust and suspect "oddballs." The family must make the child "fit" into the societal scheme of things. Education is afforded a similar role. It is most successful when it maintains the status quo, when it makes what we call "good citizens." The definition of a "good citizen" is usually one who "thinks, behaves, and responds like everyone else." Educators also feel that there is an essential body of knowledge which it is their duty to implant in each child. Their defense of this is that they are teaching "the wisdom of the ages."

To love oneself is to struggle to rediscover and maintain your uniqueness. It is understanding and appreciating the idea that you will be the only you to ever live upon this earth, that when you die so will all of your fantastic possibilities. It is the realization that even you are not totally aware of the wonders which lie dormant within yourself. Herbert Otto says only about five percent of our human potential is realized in our lifetime. Margaret Mead has hypothesized that four percent is discovered. What of the other 95 percent?

Personal Challenge

The psychiatrist R.D. Laing, has written: "We think much less than what we know, we know much less than what we love, we love much less than what there is, and to this precise extent we are much less then what we are."

There is a you, lying dormant. A potential within you to be realized. It does not matter whether you have an intelligence quotient of 60 or 160, there is more of you than what you are presently aware of. Perhaps the only peace and joy in life lies in the pursuit of and the development of this potential. It is doubtful that one will realize all of his "self" in a lifetime even if his every moment were dedicated to it.

Goethe has Faust discover this when he says, "If on this earth one moment of peace could I find, then unto that moment would I say, 'Linger awhile, so fair thou art.'" If he rests from his searches even for a brief moment, he is courting the devil, for there can be no peace in man's struggle to become. The Gospel of St. John tells us that our house has many rooms, each with its own wonders to disclose. How can we be content to let spiders, rats, decay and death take over our house?

What may be is always potential for discovery. It is never too late. This knowledge should give man his greatest challenge—the pursuit of self—his own personal Odyssey; discovering his rooms and putting them in order. It should challenge him not only to be a good person, a loving person, a feeling person, an intelligent person, but the best, most loving, feeling, intelligent person he is capable of. His search is not in competition with anyone else's. He becomes his own personal challenge.

So loving yourself involves the discovery of the true wonder of you; not only the present you, but the many possibilities of you. It involves the continual realization that you are unique, like no other person in the world, that life is, or should be, the discovery, the development and the sharing of this uniqueness. The process is not always easy, for one is bound to find those who will feel threatened by a changing, growing you. But it will always be exciting, always be fresh and like all things new and changing, never be dull. The trip into oneself is the grandest, most enjoyable and longest lasting. The fare is cheap; it merely involves continual experiencing, evaluating, educating, trying out of new behavior. Only you can be the final judge in determining what is right for you.

Valuing Ourselves

The Western culture has been a culture of competitors. The worth of a man has always been measured by how much more he has than other men. If he has a larger home, a more powerful car, a more impressive formal education, he must be a better man. But these are not universal values. There are cultures whose highest adulation goes to the holy man, the teacher, who has spent his lifetime in self-discovery and has nothing of monetary value to show for it. There are cultures who value joy and peace of mind over property and busyness. They hypothesize that since all men must die, whether poor or rich, the only real goal of life is the present joy and the realization of self in joy, not the collection of material things. There are areas where nature has taught and continues to teach this lesson with a vengeance. What good is accumulating objects or building large villas at the base of Mt. Etna? What is the purpose of permanent housing where monsoons come annually and wash away all but the people and the land?

The Thirties in the United States caused many to take a deep look at values. After the Market crash, men who had put their store in "things" went under with them, even to suicide. Other men, who had put their hope in themselves, sighed, "I did it once. I can do it again," and went out to create anew. Loving yourself involves appreciating the value of you above all things.

Loving yourself also involves the knowledge that only you can be you. If you try to be like anyone else, you may come very close, but you will always be second best. But, you are the best you. It is the easiest, most practical, most rewarding thing to be. Then it makes sense that you can only be to others what you are to yourself.

If you know, accept, and appreciate yourself and your uniqueness, you will permit others to do so. If you value and appreciate the discovery of yourself, you will encourage others to engage in self-discovery. If you recognize your need to be free to discover who you are, you will allow others their freedom to do so, also. When you realize you are the best you, you will accept the fact that others are the best they. But it follows that it all starts with you. To the extent to which you know yourself, and we are all more alike than different, you can know others. When you love yourself, you will love others. And to the depth and extent to which you can love yourself, only to that depth and extent will you be able to love others.

PART TWO

The Dynamics of Love

*The only way
you can ever hope to be loved
is to stop asking for it
and start giving it.*

Dale Carnegie

Love by itself makes light everything that is heavy, and bears evenly all that is uneven. For it carries a burden that is no burden, and everything that is bitter it makes sweet and tasteful. . . . Love feels no burden, thinks nothing of trouble, attempts what is above its strength, pleads no excuse of impossibility. . . . Though weary, it is not tired; though pressed, it is not straitened; though alarmed it is not confounded; but like a lively flame and burning torch forces its way upward and securely passes through all. . . . In whatever instance we seek ourselves, there we fall from love.

Thomas a Kempis
Of the Imitation of Christ

All the power that manifests through you comes from one Source. You open the channel for it through constant loving service, humility, and devotion. Let it always flow steadily and the current will grow mightier and mightier every day, so that whoever comes in contact with you will be blessed. It is when your heart is humble that the light of love sheds its radiance through you. That light reaches every one whose life you touch.

Swami Paramananda
Daily Thoughts and Prayers

VI

The Ways of Love

by John Powell

In the process of loving there are three important stages or moments:

    (1) Kindness: a warm assurance that "I am on your side. I care about you."

    (2) Encouragement: a strong reassurance of your own strength and self-sufficiency.

    (3) Challenge: a loving but firm exhortation to action.

It has been said that loving is an art and this means that there are no scientific-type formulae that can be applied to guarantee successful results. One must take constant readings of the relational situation and try to judge what is needed, when to apply it, and how much of it to apply. Just as an artist-painter uses canvas and oils to achieve certain desired effects, so the artist-lover must try to sense when the need is for more kindness, more encouragement, or more challenge. It is never easy.

Kindness. Someone has wisely said that "people do not care how much you know until they know how much you care." I am sure that this is the foundation of love: a communicated caring about the happiness of the one loved and an affirmation or reassurance of that loved one's worth. To build a relationship on any other foundation is to build on sand. I have to know that you really want my happiness and my growth, that you really are "for me" or I will not open at all to your influence.

I must understand that I am a person to you, not just a thing. I must know that I am not simply a "case" to be treated, or a "problem" to be solved. And so, the first thing that love must do is communicate these three things: I truly care about you. I really want your happiness, and I will do all I can to assure it. You are a uniquely valuable person.

Encouragement. For a long time in my own life, I would like to admit to you, I thought of love as doing acts of kindness for others. I even fell victim to the delusion that doing things for others which they could have and should have done for themselves was really love. If a person were painfully shy, I would leap into action, saving them from the distress involved in self-assertion. For the indecisive, I was a repository of answers. Every person who ever submitted a problem to me was immediately blessed with an instant solution. I never let others struggle long enough to win a victory for or over themselves.

Gradually the truth settled in on me. The settling in started when someone suggested to me: "Give a man a fish and he can eat for a day. Teach him to fish and he can eat for a lifetime." The application was obvious. Shy, indecisive, and struggling people may welcome or even invite us to provide for them. They may even say "I cannot" when they really mean "I do not want to put out whatever is needed." They may try various forms of manipulation to hitchhike on the stability, decisiveness, or assertiveness of others. And we average persons are tempted. We are very vulnerable, in fact, to such manipulation. It is more immediately gratifying to say, "Of course, I will do it for you," or to offer the advice, "What you really need to do is this. . . ." The right response in such cases usually provides much less immediate gratification. "Oh, come on, you can do it. . . . I do not know what you should do. You have a good mind and you are capable of making decisions. What do you think you should do?"

When we cave in and allow others to be only persons-by-proxy, we train them to need us. They have to come back to us to get their deeds done and their problems solved. We develop clienteles of progressively weaker people in need of a "fix." We train them to be addicts in need of us. It is not at all loving.

One of the hardest-to-accept facts about true love is that it is liberating. Love offers a person roots (a sense of belonging) and wings (a sense of independence and freedom). What people really need is belief in themselves, confidence in their own ability to take on the problems and opportunities of life. This is what is meant by the second stage of love: encouragement. To encourage means to put courage in. It instills into the recipient a new and fuller awareness of his or her own powers, strength, and self-sufficiency. Encouragement says: You can do it!

Challenge. The final stage of love is challenge. After conveying kindness ("I am for you!") and implanting courage ("You can do it!") true love should then invite the beloved to "stretch," to grow beyond the old limitation, to attempt what was always considered too difficult, to break a self-destructive habit that has always been too overpowering, to rise above a fear, to give up a grudge, to open a repressed feeling, to confront a difficult situation, to offer a painful apology.

If encouragement makes the one loved aware of his or her strength, challenge is the loving push to actually use this strength: "Try. Stretch. Do it. If you succeed, I will be in the front row clapping my hands off. If you fail, I will be sitting right at your side. You won't be alone. Go ahead now. Give it your best shot. You can do it!"

Love and Responsibility

Many nice, bland things can be said of love. For example, "Love divides one's burdens in half." An old monastic saying has it that "where there is love there is no labor." We sometimes roast the people we love, but we always have a toast for love: "If we only have love. . . ." Love should indeed be toasted as the secret of a full and meaningful life, but it is no favor to love to romanticize it. T. S. Eliot once remarked that "sometimes man cannot stand too much reality." And Ionesco has made the observation that "man is forever trying to turn real life into literature."

The truth about love, I think, is that it is indeed a profound comfort, but it is also a monumental challenge. Love immediately challenges me to break the fixation I have with myself. It will drag me all the way from my infantile *id* to a complete self-donation to a cause or to a person in freely given love. Love demands that I learn how to focus my attention on the needs of those I love. It will ask me to become a sensitive listener. At times love will insist that I postpone my own gratifications to meet the needs of those I love. The kind of communication which is the lifeblood of love will require me to get in touch with my most sensitive feelings and my most buried thoughts, and to share these in the frightening act of self-disclosure. Love will make me vulnerable. It will open me to the honest reactions of others whom I have allowed to penetrate my defenses. If I have built protective walls around my vulnerable places, love will tear them down.

Love will teach me to give and to receive without pan-scales. Love transcends pan-scale justice. If love divides the burdens of life in half by sharing, it also doubles one's responsibilities. Two do not eat as cheaply as one, unless one of the two does not eat. It is also true that two cannot make decisions as quickly as one. Two are not as mobile as one, and so forth.

In other words, if you do not want to—
- break the fixation with self and give up your self-centeredness,
- learn how to care about and be sincerely dedicated to the satisfaction of another,
- become a sensitive listener, who hears what is said and some things that are not able to be said,

- postpone personal gratification to meet the needs of an other,
- get in touch with your deepest feelings and most hidden thoughts,
- share your most vulnerable self as an act of love,
- get honest feedback from someone who really knows you through your own self-disclosure,
- give up your pan-scales and be prepared to give 100 per cent,
- take on the added responsibilities for a "we,"
- work at the delicate art of dialogue and shared decision making,

. . . if you do not want these things, then obviously you do not want love. If you prefer to be an island, a recluse, a narcissist, preferring to live in a world that has a population of one, love would rip out of your hands everything that you hold dear and clutch tightly.

And yet, it seems obvious to me, as I feel sure it will seem to you, that these very challenges of a true love relationship, which assault our self-centeredness, are in fact the bridge to human maturity and ultimate human fulfillment. Viktor Frankl writes:

> A thought transfixed me: for the first time in my life I saw the truth as it is set into song by so many poets, proclaimed as the final wisdom by so many thinkers. The truth—that love is the ultimate and the highest goal to which man can aspire. Then I grasped the meaning of the greatest secret that human poetry and human thought and belief have to impart: the salvation of man is through love and in love.[1]

Another great psychiatrist, Dr. Karl Menninger, liked to repeat: "Love cures. It cures those who give it and it cures those who receive it." Even the great doctors . . . are unanimous in the praise of love and love relationships as the chief source of human maturation. When Sigmund Freud was asked for a definition of mental and emotional health, he said: "It is the capacity to work and to love." Likewise, Alfred Adler said that "all human failures are the result of a lack of love." More and more psychologists are coming to esteem the capacity for intimacy. People with low capacities for love relationships are ten times more likely to be chronically ill and five times more likely to be labeled psychiatrically ill. The command of Jesus that we love one another seems to be a human imperative rather than an option. The experimental evidence for the crippling effects of a loveless life is found in the office of every psychiatrist, filled with children and adults who have no awareness of their own worth, no sense of identity, who are filled with hatred and fear and tortured by anxiety. Love is costly, but the alternatives are deadly.

The Challenges and Comforts

Michael Novak has written of marriage and family in words I would like to share with you. What he said in the following lengthy excerpt, originally published in *Harper's Magazine,* is applicable, I think, to any true commitment of love:

> In our society, of course, there is no need to become an adult. One may remain—one is daily exhorted to remain—a child forever. In such a life, the central aim is self-fulfillment. Marriage is merely an alliance, entailing as minimal an abridgement of inner privacy as one partner may allow. Children are not a welcome responsibility, for to have children is, plainly, to cease being a child oneself. One tries instead to live as the angels were once believed to live—soaring, free, unencumbered.
>
> People say of marriage that it is boring, when what they mean is that it terrifies them: too many and too deep are its searing revelations, its angers, its rages, its hates, and its loves. They say of marriage that it is deadening, when what they mean is that it drives us beyond adolescent fantasies and romantic dreams. They say of children that they are piranhas, brats, snots, when what they mean is that the importance of parents with respect to the future of their children is now known with greater clarity and exactitude than ever before.

Being married and having children has impressed on my mind certain lessons, and most of what I am forced to learn about myself is not pleasant. The quantity of sheer impenetrable selfishness in the human breast (in my breast) is a never failing source of wonderment. I do not want to be disturbed, challenged, troubled. Huge regions of myself belong only to me. Seeing myself through the unblinking eyes of an intelligent, honest spouse is humiliating. Trying to act fairly to children, each of whom is temperamentally different from myself and from each other, is baffling. My family bonds hold me back from many opportunities. And yet these bonds are, I know, my liberation. They force me to be a different sort of human being in a way I want and need.[2]

Novak goes on to say that it would be a lie to write only of the difficulties and not of the beauty of love. In fact, I think weathering the storms of the love process is the only way to find the rainbows of life. The comfort that one finds on the "less-traveled road" of love are found nowhere else. Life has a much deeper meaning when I truly love another. The loneliness of a world that has a population of one is filled by a new and warm presence when love enters a life. The self-alienation of the old person who could not interact intimately is replaced in the person renewed by love by a sense of self and of self-worth. It is what we call today a sense of "identity." It has become a truism that we can know and love only as much of ourselves as we are willing to share with another in love. The aimless wandering of the loveless person finds in love a sense of belonging and a place called home.

Going out to another in love means risk—the risks of self-disclosure, rejection, misunderstanding. It means grief, too, from the temporary separations, psychological or physical, to the final separation of death. Whoever insists on personal security and safety as the nonnegotiable conditions of life will not be willing to pay love's price or find love's enrichments. Whoever shuts himself or herself up in the cocoon of self-protective defenses, keeping others always at a safe distance and holding on tightly to personal possessions and privacy, will find the price of love far too high and will remain forever a prisoner of fear. Erich Fromm writes:

> To be loved, and to love, needs courage, the courage to judge certain values as of ultimate concern—and to take the jump and stake everything on these values.[3]

FOOTNOTES:

[1] *Man's Search for Meaning.*
[2] *The Family Out of Favor.*
[3] *The Art of Loving.*

VII

Love in Action

by Swami Chinmayananda

To give is any day nobler than to receive, and this is especially true in regards to love. When someone gives us their love it seems like the Lord is smiling upon us, and we are thankful for the love received. But our attitude throughout life should be to give love to all of the Lord's creation. This is the greatest worship we can offer Him.

Some people believe that to the extent that they give love they will become depleted, and therefore withhold their love. They do not understand that nothing else can enrich life as much as giving love to all. All other glories fade away, but the divinely sweet beauty of love given and tenderness shared remains untarnished under all circumstances. Even adversity cannot dim its brilliance nor age destroy its beauty.

Unintelligent people refuse to give love. To all intelligent people of dynamic character, however, the word "giving" has a different meaning, and every one of these actions provides them with more inspiration. To give is to them an expression of their creativity and mastery, of their strength, power, wealth, and efficiency. It is the very inspiration in their living, the very breath of their existence. To such people giving love is the noblest expression of their own personality. In the act-of-giving they experience true joy and complete self-fulfillment.

To give love is to expand. Then the lover functions from two centers: from within himself, and from the beloved, a center outside himself. Thus, the happiness of a true giver of love increases, and his sense of loneliness departs. For when we give love to all we not only lose our sense of separateness, but we feel good that we are making the world indebted to us, rather than getting ourselves indebted to the world. We are the givers of love, the creditors; the creatures around us are the recipients, the debtors. To receive love is to be forever indebted to the world.

This "giving of love" must be a natural outpouring, as natural as the bird singing in the springtime, the moonlight comforting the earth, or a mother giving her milk to her child. A natural, effortless, joyous giving must be our outpouring of love unto the world around us.

The poor cannot give because they have nothing to give. But one who is wealthy and still does not give because of his attachments is also poor. One who has love and does not give it, but demands more love from others can never be rich. He is a "miser," (kṛpaṇaḥ) as the term is used in the Gītā and Upanishads.

When I say "give," I do not mean wealth or physical strength or power. If we have enough we must give these also as an expression of our love, but to give love is to give a part of our own life, to share our joy, knowledge, and courage.

This giving is not to be polluted by the vaguest trace of expectation to receive anything in return. Here the giving of love, in itself, is its own reward and happiness. The spontaneity of such happiness enhances the intensity and depth of satisfaction in it.

Such a dynamic expression of love transforms both the giver and the receiver. Give freely and amply of yourself. Imitate the splendor of a solitary flower sweetening the neighborhood even if it blossoms on a lonely peak!

In such a lavish giving of love the fusion of ourselves with the world can take place, and through this self-unfoldment our sense of separateness ends. Herein lies the wondrous joy of a total freedom from loneliness, fear, anxiety, and mental depression.

Remember, even a little giving of oneself is an expression of true love. The mother's love for the child, the child's love for his parents, a person's love for his country, or community, and a devotee's love for the Lord—are all expressed in self-sacrifice.

If we have not cultivated these capacities we can never be successful in love. We often hear people complain: "I did so much for him—I fed him, clothed him, protected him—yet, he has no love for me now." It is indeed one of the most painful of worldly experiences if our friends and relatives do not reciprocate or appreciate our love. But the cause is mainly in ourselves, as we have not given our love freely enough.

The Dynamic Elements of Love

In all forms of love there are some fundamental factors besides the act of giving. These dynamic elements must always be in the heart of the lover. Otherwise, the love manifested is false; it will only be an illusion of love. Such an impotent love cannot produce any blessings, neither for the giver nor for the recipient. There are four factors that go into the constitution of love which form the basis for enduring and productive love:

    (i)   A sincere concern for the beloved,

    (ii) A sense of deep response,

    (iii) An ardent attitude of reverence, and

    (iv) A complete understanding of the beloved.

These four factors are always valid, whether we are loving the world, or whether our love is turned toward the Lord of the universe. Sometimes we sincerely believe that we have given love, but we fail to feel the exhilarating joy promised by the great masters. Then we feel extremely disappointed, and think that we have been cheated.

But a sufficient quantity of sincere love, when given unreservedly, can never go unrewarded. Where Godlike love is given, joy must follow. We can develop and direct the outward flow of love from ourselves by being mindful of all these above-mentioned basic factors. When they are present then our love is complete, potent, and sincere. Let us now examine each of these.

Sincere Concern

A sincere concern for the well-being of the beloved is the first essential factor of love. A mother who loves her children is always anxious for their happiness. Similarly, if one loves flowers, a pet, or one's country, then one will also be greatly concerned for their well-being.

If, for example, we claim to love our plants but we forget to water them, then it is not true love. We cannot claim to love animals and then mistreat them, or say that we love our parents and then be insensitive to their needs. When love exists, we become immediately and automatically anxious for the happiness of the beloved. In the happiness of the beloved we feel extremely happy, and to a true lover no sacrifice is too great if it is in the best interest of the beloved.

A true lover of one's country will suffer, go to war, or live in poverty if that will bring prosperity and glory to his or her country. Where there is true love, the lover is never tired of working for and serving the beloved. A loving teacher never tires of teaching. A loving mother never gets tired of working for her children and their father. A sincere lover of the nation serves the cause of the country day and night. Love and action go hand in hand. One readily strives for that which one loves. And one really loves that for which one labors wholeheartedly. Where there is love, labor becomes a joy.

Therefore, when you love, always be ready to serve the beloved, and work for the beloved's cause. Merely saying "I love," is not sufficient, we must express our love in action. That is much more noble, compelling, and dynamic. Let your hands and legs serve, but do not speak about love. Flood the atmosphere with your heartfelt love. You will then be creating an enchanting magic around you causing everyone to love you.

Deep Response

Secondly, the lover will always have a sense of deep response to the beloved. When one is sincerely concerned for the beloved, the ability to respond readily to their needs and feelings will rise in the lover's mind. This "ability to respond" is the true meaning of the word response(a)bility. However, this term is often misunderstood as some burdensome duty being imposed upon us by some power outside ourselves. But as we grow and expand in love we become more sensitive to the silent needs of others, and trying to satisfy their needs becomes a lover's ecstatic passion.

This is most conspicuously seen in a mother. Her love for her children is immeasurable. She is so in tune with them that even when they are far away she intuitively knows when they are not well. This is known as "telepathy" in psychology. This secret ability to respond with sympathy to the beloved always exists in the heart of a true lover. This is true only when there is deep and sincere love, otherwise we feel only our own selfish wish. Give love, and be sensitive in your heart to the unspoken wishes of the beloved. You will find that this actually happens many times a day. These instances not only surprise you, but they especially thrill the beloved. Each time it happens, there will be an explosion of joy in the hearts of the lover and the beloved.

Leaders become popular, business men become more successful, people become great, all because of an instinctive ability to tune into the needs of others. In all such cases they naturally have an natural intense love for others or their work.

These are two of the four basic factors behind love. One cannot exist without the other. They are both intimately connected with each other. We can never have "sincere concern" for, without "a sense of deep response" to the beloved.

Attitude of Reverence

The divine faculty of effortlessly knowing the feelings and needs of others can never be generated in full measure unless we have the third factor of true love—an ardent attitude of reverence.

We generally meet the world only from the surface of our personality and not from its depth. When we operate from a superficial level, we can contact others only at that level. If we delve deeper into our own inner nature, however, we can also contact the deeper level in others. For example, with our eyes we can see others, with our hands we can physically contact others, but only from our hearts can we touch the hearts of others and evoke their empathy and compassion. With our thoughts we can kindle new thoughts in others and therein unveil new understanding. Thus, to contact the depth in others we must learn to express love from the deeper depths within ourselves.

Reverence is not merely an emotion of love from the heart, or respect due to an intellectual understanding. We can love without respect and we can also respect without loving. We can love chocolate without understanding its ingredients or how it is made. We may understand science and therefore we respect scientists, but that does not necessarily mean that we love every scientist.

The feeling that is generated when a sense of love from the mind and respect from the intellect merge at one and the same altar is called "reverence." This can take place only with an integrated mind and intellect.

Our love for others becomes potent when we have a deep sense of reverence for life and all living creatures. Our loving approaches will certainly be rebuked if we have no respect for others. Loving the world without reverence for life and people is like a beautiful curry, well cooked and nicely served, but without salt!

Of the factors in reverence, the love-aspect is commonly

known to us. We tend to misinterpret the word "respect," however, attaching to it a feeling mingled with fear and awe, thereby
distancing ourselves from the object of our reverence. This is
not correct, as the root from which the word "respect" comes is
respicere meaning "to look at." To respect people means to *recognize* them as they are. To show respect is to help them grow
and unfold themselves, in themselves, by themselves. Parents
should respect their children, and teachers must have respect for
their students.

True respect is often lacking in our relationships because
what we call love is an attempt to make use of the beloved for
our own purposes. Thus, we try to make them conform to the
way we want them to be. This is not love. A true lover sees the
beloved with perfect objectivity, and without interfering with
the personality of the beloved, blesses him or her to grow and
unfold. Thus, pure love has a revitalizing effect upon others. In
the presence of such a truly loving person, others grow and expand into a healthier state of being. Without deep reverence for
the beloved such a refreshing stream of love cannot flow from
the heart of the lover.

Most of us need help to function efficiently as a psychological entity. Rarely, if ever, are we free in our mental life. We need
sympathy, applause, acceptance, and kindness from others to
support our individuality, our ego. In short, we want to be loved
by others.

To give love we must become independent in ourselves and
be a pillar in life for others to hold onto. Only one who needs no
crutches for his own existence has the power to give love. All
others are receivers of love. One who has such an inner strength
of personality, and a deep reverence for life and people comes to
give love, and thereby transforms the world of creatures in his
orbit. He becomes an island of peace and contentment in the
stormy life of turbulent fears and shattering confusions around
him.

Inner Expansion

The ardent attitude of reverence can arise only where there is full understanding. Therefore, the fourth basic factor in love is "a complete understanding of the beloved." Without reverence the response will not be satisfactory, and where there is no ability to respond there can be no deep concern for the beloved. Concern for, and response and reverence to the beloved can only be true if they flow from a firm and sure understanding of the beloved thing or being.

In *Narada Bhakti Sutra* (the Hindu treatise on Divine Love), the means for developing divine love have been described. The very first sutra in this discussion says, "Some say understanding alone is the means." (Sutra 28) This is true. Without a general knowledge of the object of our love we cannot feel love. With deeper understanding, our love also expands. Superficial knowledge is not sufficient. What is necessary is an understanding that pierces through the outer layers and penetrates into the core of the beloved's personality. Only this type of understanding assures a steady reverence, quick response, and a real concern for the "object" of our love.

To pierce into the depth of another, we must lose our selfishness, and learn to be one with the beloved—be it a community, nation, or the world. As long as we remain overly concerned with our own physical comforts we can never effectively give love. We need to expand into the greater and nobler spiritual dimensions within ourselves. In this inner expansion alone can the sense of separateness with its suffocating sorrows, fears and anxieties end.

The analytical methods of modern physiology and psychology cannot reach these depths. They are not capable of unraveling the mystery of man's personality. Using these methods we understand each other with physical, mental, and intellectual information based on perceptions which are largely vague and erroneous. To reach the depths of our being, love alone is the means, the path. It alone has the necessary penetration to reach the required depth to discover the real Essence—the one infinite Self—in ourselves and others.

Until we discover this spiritual Center in ourselves, the God in us, we will be confused and disturbed, an enigma to ourselves and to others. From the Self alone all is known in its entirety, and it is only with reference to It that we can correctly perceive the relative positions of all other factors in our personality. This understanding can come to us only through the words of the great rishis and by consistently applying and developing our present ability to love others.

Without love we make a hell of this world; with true love this world becomes a heaven. To give love we must have the rich treasure of all these four fundamental factors of love. Ultimately true love helps my understanding of myself and the world around me. The Self in me is the Self everywhere.

VIII

The Prayer of St. Francis

by Eknath Easwaran

Lord, make me an instrument of thy peace.
Where there is hatred, let me sow love;
Where there is injury, pardon;
Where there is doubt, faith;
Where there is despair, hope;
Where there is darkness, light;
Where there is sadness, joy;

O Divine Master, grant that I may not so much seek
To be consoled as to console,
To be understood as to understand,
To be loved as to love:
For it is in giving that we receive,
It is in pardoning that we are pardoned,
It is in dying to self that we are born to eternal life.

When I first came to this country about twenty-five years ago, I looked hard for a suitable meditation passage for the West. In this Prayer of Saint Francis I found the perfect answer. During all these years I have been recommending it to everyone because, as you can see, it is a very rare thing: an attempt to reverse almost all the ordinary tendencies we find in human nature. It gives us a blueprint for making our life a blessing for everyone.

In this profoundest of prayers, Saint Francis confides in us how the son of Pietro di Bernardone was transformed into a son of God. We too can aspire to such a transformation by making his Prayer an integral part of our consciousness. This cannot be done through reading or discussion, which take place only on the surface level of consciousness. It can only be done by regular, systematic meditation. If we meditate on Saint Francis's words diligently and with enthusiasm every morning, the marvelous transformation that Francis worked in himself will gradually be effected in us too.

This word "meditation" means many different things to different people. It has been applied to dancing and to listening to music and even to letting the mind wander, which is just the opposite of meditation. I want to explain right from the outset that when I talk about meditation, I mean only one thing: systematically training the mind to focus completely on a lofty ideal until that ideal absorbs our every faculty and passion. In the West this focusing of the mind is often called "interior prayer" or "contemplation," the word "meditation" being used for a kind of disciplined reflection on a single religious theme (such as the Passion) and its significance. But whatever term is used, the practice I am referring to is universal. It has been described in every major spiritual tradition. If you look at the writings of early figures of Christianity like the Desert Fathers, I think you will agree that they would immediately recognize the method I myself follow and teach.

For those who are not familiar with this method, a brief summary will clarify the references to meditation I make throughout the rest of this article.

Instructions in Meditation

Begin by devoting half an hour every morning as early as convenient to the practice of meditation. If you want to meditate more, have half an hour in the evening also, but do not meditate longer than half an hour at a time.

If you do not have a meditation room in your home, a special corner set aside for that purpose will do. Whichever you choose, your meditation place should be quiet. Keep it simple and attractive with a few religious pictures if they appeal to you.

Sit in a straight-backed chair—one with arms—or cross-legged on the floor, with spinal column erect and eyes gently closed. As your concentration deepens, you may begin to relax and fall asleep. If so, draw yourself up and move away from your back support so that you can keep spine, neck, and head in a straight line.

To meditate on the Prayer of Saint Francis, you will need to know the words by heart. (Until you learn them, you can begin with a passage from Scripture that you already know, such as the Lord's Prayer or the Twenty-third Psalm.) Go through the words in your mind as slowly as you can, letting each word drop singly into your consciousness like a jewel. Do not follow any association of ideas, but keep to the words of the Prayer. If you are giving them your full attention, you do not have to turn them over in your mind; the meaning cannot help sinking in. Similarly, when distractions come, do not resist them; that way they will seize your attention. Instead, simply try to give more and more attention to the words of the Prayer.

It is said that once Saint Francis carved a small cup and was so pleased with his handiwork that his eyes kept wandering back to it even during prayer. When suddenly he realized that the cup was taking his thoughts away from God, he picked it up and flung it into the fire. We do not need to be that severe with ourselves, but if you find that your mind has wandered completely away from the Prayer, just go back to the first word of that stanza and begin again. Adding to your repertoire of inspirational passages from the scriptures or great mystics will help to keep the words of the passage from growing stale.

After long and strenuous endeavor, the day will come when the windows of your senses close down completely and you are able to meditate with one-pointed absorption on the Prayer. Saint Teresa of Avila described this stage vividly:

> You will at once feel your senses gather themselves together; they seem like bees which return to the hive and then shut themselves up to work at the making of honey; and this will take place without effort or care on your part. God thus rewards the violence which your soul has been doing to itself, and gives to it such a domination over the senses that a sign is enough, when it desires to recollect itself, for them to obey and so gather themselves together. At the first call of the will they come back more and more quickly. At last, after many and many exercises of this kind, God disposes them to a state of absolute repose and of perfect contemplation.

In the book [*Love Never Faileth*] I try to give practical commentary on passages for meditation from four great Christian exponents of what I call "love in action." My hope is to make these passages more meaningful for those who want to meditate on them and then translate their ideals into action. But although I often comment line for line, let me repeat that what I am recommending you do in meditation is very different. When you go through these words in meditation, your mind will want to follow all kinds of associations. This is not getting absorbed in the Prayer; it is wandering away from it. As you meditate on these precious words, give them all your attention. Gradually they will become part of you, reflected in everything you say and do.

The central principle of meditation is that we become what we meditate on. Over time, the transformation taking place in our character and consciousness is bound to show itself in our daily relations. Part of this transformation is accomplished in meditation, but the rest is done during the day. Meditation generates power that needs to be put to constructive use, particularly in healing our relationships. Francis once said that we pray to partake of the peace of the Lord, but that the hours of the day are meant for spreading this peace in the places where people dwell. When things go wrong at home, for instance, we need to try to remain patient and sympathetic. When someone at work is curt to us, we need to harness the strength found in meditation to move closer and show that person some special kindness.

The Holy Name

To do this, it is a great help to learn to use the Holy Name—a powerful spiritual formula which, when repeated silently in the mind, has the power to transform consciousness. There is nothing magical about this power; it is simply a matter of practice, as you can verify for yourself.

Repetition of the Holy Name is a practice found in every major religious tradition. Many Christians simply repeat *Jesus, Jesus, Jesus*. The Desert Fathers repeated the Prayer of Jesus, which some Eastern Orthodox Christians use even today: *Lord, Jesus Christ, have mercy upon me*. Catholics use *Hail Mary* or *Ave Maria*, and one Catholic monastic friend has written to inform me that she uses an ancient Aramaic formula: *Maranatha*, "Come, Lord Jesus." Choose whichever version of the Holy Name appeals to you; then, once you have chosen, stick to that and do not change. Otherwise you will be like a person digging little holes in many places; you will never go deep enough to find water.

Repeat the Holy Name whenever you get the chance: while walking, while waiting, while doing mechanical chores like washing dishes, and especially when you are falling asleep, anytime you are not doing something that requires your attention. Whenever you are angry or afraid, nervous or hurried or resentful, repeat the Holy Name until the agitation in your mind subsides. All these states of mind are power running against you, which the Holy Name can harness and put to work.

I might mention that not just any phrase has this power. By and large, it is good not to make up your own version of the Holy Name but to use a formula that has been sanctioned by centuries of devout tradition. Most words and phrases denote something to us only at relatively superficial levels of awareness; below that, in the unconscious, they mean nothing. If you repeat the Holy Name sincerely and systematically, however, you can verify for yourself that it goes deeper with every repetition. It can be with you even in the uttermost depths of your consciousness, as you will discover for yourself when you find it reverberating in a dream—or, deeper still, during dreamless sleep. When you awake, the thrill of this great experience will remain with you, reminding and inspiring and enabling you to be a little calmer and kinder throughout that day.

In the case of Saint Francis, we find this practice arising spontaneously from the depths of his ardent love. The *Fioretti* or *Little Flowers of Saint Francis*, the earliest collection we have of stories about Francis and the early Order, relates that the nobleman Bernard of Quintavalle, before he enlisted himself as a disciple, wanted to find out for himself whether young Francis of Assisi was a sincere lover of God; so he invited him to his wealthy home. "Saint Francis accepted the invitation," the chronicle continues,

> and took supper with him, and stayed the night also; and then Bernard resolved to make trial of his sanctity. He got a bed prepared for him in his own room, in which a lamp was always burning all night. Saint Francis, in order to conceal his sanctity, entered the room and immediately threw himself on the bed and feigned to sleep. Bernard also resolved to lie down, and began to snore loudly, as if in a very deep slumber.
> Thereupon Saint Francis, believing that Bernard was really asleep, immediately rose from the bed and betook himself to prayer, and raising his eyes and his hands to heaven with the greatest devotion he said, My God and my all!" So saying, and shedding many tears, he remained until morning, constantly repeating "My God and my all!" and nothing more.

Meditation and the repetition of the Holy Name go hand in hand: meditation is for the quiet hours of morning and evening; the Holy Name can be used at any other time of day or night.

Together these two help us to change negative habits at a depth our ordinary will cannot reach. Francis once said that our knowledge is as deep as our action. Many people are victims of habits, such as smoking or drinking, which they know to be harmful, but still they are unable to give them up. If this knowledge is driven deeper into their consciousness through meditation and the Holy Name, it can free them from the tyranny of undesirable habits to follow wiser patterns of behavior.

One of Francis's contemporaries, a historian who had been a student at Bologna and heard Francis speak on the Feast of the Assumption, described him in this way:

> His habit was dirty, his appearance insignificant, his face not handsome. But God gave his words such power that many noble families, between whom there had been much old-time enmity and spilled blood, allowed themselves to be induced to make peace. And all felt great devotion and reverence for him. . . . He was not silent about wrongs that he saw, but gave everything its right name. And it seemed to each who listened that the poor little man from Assisi talked to him alone, as if all the words he heard were directed to him, and one after another, like well-aimed arrows sent by a master hand, thrust their points into his heart.

This is precisely what we experience in meditation as the holy words of Saint Francis's Prayer penetrate our hearts.

Let me now try to bring out some of the practical profundity of these words, drawing on my own experience of their power.

Lord make me an instrument of thy peace

Without spending a single moment beating about the bush, Francis comes straight to the point of the spiritual life: Lord, make me an instrument of thy peace. Our first priority is to reform ourselves; without that, how can we expect to help other people reform themselves? It is the living example of a man or woman giving every moment to making love a reality that moves our hearts to follow. We do not have to call ourselves religious to serve as examples of love and unity. We do not need a bumper sticker that says, "You are following an instrument of the Lord." Our everyday actions speak for themselves.

Just as the example of Jesus inspired Francis a millennium later, Francis inspired thousands of people even during his own lifetime. Near the end of his life, while he was making a mountain journey, Francis's health failed. His companions went into a farmyard to borrow a donkey for him to ride. On hearing for whom it was intended, the peasant came out and asked, "Are you the Brother Francis there is so much said about?" Receiving a nod from one of Francis's companions, he added, "Then take care that you are as good in reality as they say, for there are many who have confidence in you." Deeply stirred, Francis kissed the peasant in gratitude for this reminder of just how much such an example could mean even to people he had never met.

How can we go about making ourselves such an example? To begin with, as long as we are full of ourselves, our own small desires and self-centered thoughts, we leave no room whatever for the Lord to work in our lives. Jesus says simply, "Thy will be done." The implication is clear: to live in harmony with the divine will, our petty, selfish, personal will—self-will—has to go. When we ask to be made instruments of peace, what we are really asking for is the boundless determination to empty ourselves of every ugly state of mind that disrupts relationships— anger, resentment, jealousy, greed, self-will in any form.

Transforming these negative states of mind into their positive counterparts is not at all an easy task. Selfish desires and resentments seem to slip right through our fingers. They give us no handhold, nothing to clutch at. That is the challenge. If we could pick up anger like a pebble and throw it where it could never bother us again, the chances of developing a strong will would be extremely slim. Yet without a will that cannot be broken, we cannot fight the enemy that hides behind these negative screens, not allowing us to see his ugly face. This is the ego, the source of all our selfish and destructive behavior.

In English fiction there is a fascinating character known as the Scarlet Pimpernel. He shows up here, then there, then here again, breaking the law for what he considers worthy causes, but the authorities can never lay eyes on him. That is how the ego behaves. It simply is not possible to challenge him to a duel. He will not reply to your invitation; he will never pick up your gauntlet; if you shout at him, your echo will shout back at you. But here are a million little ways in which you can slowly track the ego to its lair.

If someone were to pull over to the side of the road in San Francisco and ask me how to get to Los Angeles, I would not say, "Go north." Everyone knows you have to go the other direction. Similarly, spiritual figures like Saint Francis tell us, "Do not follow your selfish desires and angry impulses; that is the way to emotional bankruptcy." But we reply, "Oh, no! I know what I am doing. It is obvious which way is better." Francis would insist, "Please believe me. If you go that way, you will become more insecure. People will slowly lose their respect for you, and you will lose respect for yourself. Eventually you will not feel at home anywhere on earth. Instead, let me show you a secret trail that will take you slowly round so you can surprise the ego in his sleep. He will never know what hit him."

Like most people I have met in this country, I too was conditioned at an early age by talk about not "repressing" the ego. I believed that if you defy a strong selfish impulse, sooner or later your frustrations will explode. The lives of men and women like Saint Francis, however, show us just the opposite: reducing the ego for the sake of fulfilling a higher goal, a loftier desire than self-interest, is not repression but transformation. The signs are sure. Repression bottles up our energy, so that it can make itself felt only in destructive ways. When this energy is transformed, however, it is released every day in creative ways that we can see: patience, resilience under stress, skill in building bridges between others and ourselves. When a selfish urge is crying out for satisfaction, then, that is an ideal opportunity to summon up your will and go against that urge. Because so much of our vital energy is caught up in pampering these selfish impulses, they offer us a long, long trail right into the depths of consciousness. When we defy the impulse and use its energy for some selfless purpose, we are following a trail that will eventually allow us to get around the ego.

These are the dynamics of spiritual transformation. The route is always there and it is always open; that is its promise. We must be prepared for many, many years of arduous hiking over rough terrain. Very likely we are going to have lapses; some very attractive detours may distract us temporarily. All that we are asking the Lord for is the determination to do our best to stay on the right trail and go forward.

As a practical first step toward becoming "an instrument of peace," we can try our best not to harbor grudges. One suggestion is that when you have a falling-out with someone, instead of deciding on the spot that you are not going to come within ten feet of that person, try going out for a really fast walk, repeating the Holy Name in your mind until the immediate wave of anger rolls over you. (If a fast walk is not feasible, sit down quietly to repeat the Name.) Then you can make a simple effort to recall some of the good things that person has done for you. He may have let it go by when you said something particularly unkind to him at one time; or perhaps when you got sick she took care of you. Anger makes us utterly forget all these incidents, so that for a while we see only the dark side. When we remind ourselves that even though at present we may be nursing a very real injury, the past has brought us kindness and aid from this person, our anger will find it difficult to burn for very long.

On another front, I have come to feel that one of the cornerstones of peaceful relations everywhere is the capacity to avoid becoming wedded to one's own opinions. Francis repeatedly warned his brothers about trying to "embrace poverty while keeping the purse of your own opinion." When we do not have this capacity, arrogance often makes its ugly appearance. At the mere hint of disagreement we get agitated, and our views are liable to come out clothed in harsh tones and intemperate language. The message to the other party is clear: we have scant respect for him or her as a person. Nothing wounds more deeply or muddies the original issue more thoroughly. It is then that war breaks out. We need not think of war only in terms of the War of the Roses or the landing on the beaches of Normandy. Skirmishes are fought in the dining room all the time; guerrilla warfare is often waged in the kitchen.

Where there is hatred, let me sow love

To the south of my ancestral home in Kerala, South India, beautiful rice fields stretch almost to the horizon. When I was a little boy, every morning during the planting season I would be awakened just after dawn by the sounds of the villagers plowing the land with their bullocks, talking and singing as they worked. First the tiny seedlings must be planted. Somebody goes along with a big basket, planting them one by one in a row, so carefully that when you look at rice growing, it looks like a gigantic green carpet. Later each seedling must be transplanted. All in all, it is difficult to believe that these minute seedlings are going to bear such a rich harvest.

You and I can go in for a similar kind of hand labor. When you plant just one kind word with somebody who has been unkind to you, though it is only a tiny seedling, it is going to bear a rich harvest. A lot of people get the benefit—second hand, third hand, fourth hand—from our little kindnesses. Every time you focus on what brings people together instead of what drives them apart, you are planting a long row of these seedlings. Every day—in the office, at school, in the kitchen, at the store—everyone has opportunities for this kind of hand labor. We may think our opportunities are hardly worth the trouble, but little things like kindness catch on and spread.

In Kerala we have a giant, fierce-looking plant called elephant nettle. It seems to flourish in every nook and cranny, and you have only to walk by for it to stretch out to touch you. One little touch and you feel as if you have been stung. By the time you get home, you have a blister that won't let you think about anything else until it goes away.

My Grandmother, my spiritual teacher, was expert at driving home great truths with homely illustrations. She used to say, "A self-willed person is like an elephant nettle." That is why the moment we see somebody who is given to saying unkind things, we make a detour. We pretend we have just remembered something that takes us in another direction, but the fact is that we just do not want to be stung. "I promise not to go near the elephant nettles," I always assured my Granny. But when it came to a classmate I did not like, she would say, "Here, you have to learn to grow. Go near him. Let yourself slowly get comfortable around him; then give him your sympathy and help take the sting out of his nettleness."

I am not one of those philosophical people who say, "No matter what you do to me, it is all right." Certainly not! When someone is being unkind, whether to me or to somebody else, I feel a loving obligation to remonstrate with him, kindly but firmly. When a person senses that we have his best interests at heart, when he knows we will not move away from him whatever distress he is causing, we can remonstrate and at the same time support him in his efforts to overcome his problem.

Where there is injury, pardon

When children cry, my mother used to remind me, they are really trying to speak to us. They have some problem and do not know how to explain what is bothering them, so they use the only language they have: lifting the roof off. Grown-ups usually go in for a more subtle style. When they get really annoyed, they let loose with some choice epithets, stalk out of the house (often tripping over the threshold), and growl something rude to the first person they see. We understand this more easily than an infant's tantrum, but it is just as childish. When a baby raises the roof, most people do not respond by taking it personally and getting hostile; they try to find out what the problem is and solve it. Saint Francis is reminding us that there is no more reason to take grown-ups' annoyance personally than we do children's.

No one would claim for a second that this kind of response comes easily. Dealing with acrimonious situations and self-willed people with a calm patience requires toughness, the inner toughness that real love demands. In matters like these, one of Francis's earliest disciples, Brother Juniper, won a reputation for his naive ingenuity. Once, when a superior reprimanded him with great severity, Brother Juniper was so disturbed by the grief he had caused that in the middle of the night he jumped out of bed, prepared some porridge with a big lump of butter on top, and took it to his superior's room. "Father," he said, standing at the door with the bowl of porridge in one hand and a lighted candle in the other, "today when you reprimanded me I noticed that you were hoarse from excitement. Now I have prepared this porridge for you and beg you to eat it; it is good for the throat and chest."

The superior impatiently told Brother Juniper to go away and let him sleep.

"Well," said Brother Juniper simply, "the porridge is cooked and has to be eaten, so please be so kind as to hold the light while I do the eating." His superior must have laughed in spite of himself, and we are told that he was sporting enough to sit down with Brother Juniper so they could eat the porridge together.

Most of us will never be so ingenuous as Brother Juniper, but we can still learn to head off resentment in every way possible. The more resentment is allowed to grow, the more damage it is going to do. Resentment is like swallowing a seed from the elephant nettle: soon our whole insides will ache from top to bottom from its stinging, and we won't have the vaguest idea how to get rid of it. Just think about the comparison a little. Not only will that resentment wreak havoc with our emotional well-being, it will gradually break down the functioning of our physical system as well.

Resentment will defend itself with a foolish argument: "Well, it is my own business." Not at all. In the first place, unless the person against whom you nurse the grudge is extremely secure, you are making that person into an agitated missile who is going to injure a lot of others. This is no exaggeration. Resentment is contagious, much more so than a virus. In a home where it is allowed to fester, everybody gets infected: the children, the children's playmates, even the dog. But kindness is even more contagious. Whenever people see somebody facing harsh treatment with quiet security, with a kind of infectious good humor, they get infected too. "How I wish I could do that!" they marvel. We can use kindness to inoculate those around us against the dread disease of resentment.

Where there is doubt, faith; where there is despair, hope

I keep up with a variety of magazines and newspapers, and what I find is a lot of people throwing up their hands. Many tell us all the ways the world is doomed; some insist that we cannot possibly make it into the next century. I am not one of those who claim all is well no matter what is happening. On many fronts, the horizon *is* dark. But we might well ask ourselves the question: who is responsible for the precarious nuclear stalemate, the environmental crises, the merciless exploitation of other people's resources? Not the three Greek sisters of fate. Not the force which created us. It is we ourselves who are totally responsible; therefore it is we ourselves who can set these wrong situations right.

The shining examples of Saint Francis and other spiritual figures stand as monuments of hope. They had to face adversities of every description, opposition from every imaginable kind of entrenched self-interest. Often they were able to make use of such problems to spur themselves on. When we take a good look at the state of the world, we are sometimes inclined to say, "There is nothing to be done." If we would only turn to the example of Saint Francis we would have to admit, "It's not impossible, really. Look what he was able to accomplish. Why can't we manage some of the same?"

When I was in India, I came across a number of American expressions which baffled me. One was "pulling yourself up by your own bootstraps." I resolved that when I came to this country, I would look for some person performing this acrobatic feat! This is the marvel of meditation—a marvel I have never been able to get over. Nobody pulls you up; you pull yourself up. It should appeal enormously to the justly lauded spirit of Yankee ingenuity. Francis himself said, "More than all grace and all the gifts of the Holy Ghost . . . is the conquering of yourself." You go to work on your own mind and change whatever needs changing, making yourself into the kind of person most suited to meeting the challenges of the day. There is cause for enormous hope here.

None of us need be ashamed or embarrassed if ghosts out of our past come and whisper, "Remember what you did in high school? All the escapades you took part in? How unkind you were, how you wasted so many opportunities?" To me, this sort of guilt is a trick the ego plays to make us doubt ourselves. It is most unfair. Here we are looking back at our behavior of ten or twenty or thirty years ago and judging it by our standards of today. Who has not made mistakes at some tumultuous period in life? If you ask me personally, "Did you?" I will say, "Plenty." And if you ask, "Well, don't you too feel guilty about what you did?" I will say, "I am not proud of it, but that is how I saw life then."

If you want to judge yourself, the only fair way is to judge yourself with today's eyes as you are today. Look at yourself straight on and ask, "Have I been selfish today in any way?" If you have a competitive streak, this is where you can make good use of it. Just say, "Today in such and such ways I have been somewhat selfish, but tomorrow I'll do better."

Where there is darkness, light

On a dark night when you are stumbling along the road trying to pick your way home, what would you say if somebody came up and offered to help with a flashlight that has no battery? People who are quick to anger or who nurse grudges have no battery in their flashlight; we would do well to tell them, "Please do not bring your flashdark here." Isn't there a battery called Eveready? Well, resentful people have a battery that can be called Neveready. By refusing to let their compassion shine, they darken the path of everyone around them. On the other hand, people who are patient and who can love you more than they love themselves have a flashlight that shines in all directions at the same time.

There are many different sizes of flashlights. I have one by my bedside which is the size of a fountain pen. I can hardly see anything with it, but it is better than the dark; at least it shows you where the walls are so that you avoid walking into them and banging your head. That is the first stage of our transformation: we appear as little fountain pens of light. A group at a party is saying, "I cannot see any good in Ebenezer at all," and we chime in, "Oh, he has helped me out a few times."

As we are able to work more comfortably and harmoniously with people, we will find that instead of a penlight we hold a normal, hand-sized flashlight. People begin to look to us for advice and solace. They like to be around us because we somehow make them feel more secure. Finally, when we see the spark of divinity burning in the people around us, we are like a big beacon. People are drawn to us, because they find that by our light their paths become clear and well marked.

Where there is sadness, joy

This line touches me deeply. Saint Francis is quietly bringing home to us a tremendous responsibility. Our influence,
whether for sadness or for joy, reaches everywhere. We cannot
ever say, "I live alone in an attic off Fourth Street. This line does
not apply to me." Don't you ride on a bus where thirty people see
how solemn and sad you look? Everywhere we go we affect
people.

Once a student of mine in India thought he had found an
answer to this. I met him on campus and said to him casually, "I
have been noticing how downcast you look these days. It grieves
me. Is there anything I can do?"

"There is no need for you to be concerned about the way I
look," he replied politely enough. "It is my face."

"Yes," I agreed, "it is your face. But it is we who have to
look at it!"

Francis himself was far from being a solemn-faced ascetic.
Often he went about singing softly, and on the road he liked to
regale his companions with songs of God's glories which he
composed himself—in French, the language of the troubadours.
"We Friars Minor," he exclaimed once, "what are we except
God's singers and players, who seek to draw hearts upwards and
to fill them with spiritual joy?" Their joy was so great that
"when they returned from their work at evening time or when in
the course of the day met on the road, love and joy shone out of
their eyes, and they greeted each other with chaste embraces,
holy kisses, cheerful words, modest smiles. . . . "

O Divine Master

Francis's second stanza begins beautifully: O Divine Master. . . We can all think of ourselves as the Lord's footmen and
handmaids; he is the Master, the one and only boss. It is a super-
stition to believe that we are unemployed at any time. We are all

born with our appointment orders: "You, Morton E. Hazelby, are hereby instructed to contribute to life on earth and continue contributing until the last breath of the life I have given you is spent." Those of us who take the terms of this order to heart become secure and respected wherever we go.

The ideal of living as the Lord's servant was embodied with consummate grace by Francis's dear disciple Clare. Though she held the office of abbess and all the Sisters at the tiny San Damiano convent looked up to her as their spiritual leader, it was Clare who most often served them at table, pouring water over their hands and waiting upon them. She took personal care of any Brothers and Sisters who happened to be sick, and did not hesitate to take on any chore, however lowly, that needed doing. When Sisters came home from working outside the convent, Clare washed their feet with her holy hands. And at night she often got up to put the covers back on a Sister who had uncovered herself in her sleep, for fear she might become chilled.

*Grant that I may not so much seek to be consoled
as to console*

Beggars, lepers, all who suffered were sacred in Saint Francis's eyes. Whatever he had he would willingly give to someone more in need. Often he gave away his hood, a part of his habit, or even his trousers to beggars, so that his companions had their work cut out for them just keeping clothes on their beloved Francis's back. But there was a deeper object in his giving too. One day in Perugia he met a man he had formerly known who was now reduced to utter poverty. The man complained with great bitterness at having been treated so unjustly by his master. "I will willingly give you my hood," begged Francis, "if you will forgive your master his injustice." The man's heart was moved. He forgot his hatred, it is said, and was filled with the sweetness of forgiveness.

As a boy, when I was feeling sorry for myself because of difficulties in school or with someone in the village, my Grandmother used to tell me gently, "This is not sorrow; this is self-pity. Self-pity weakens, but sorrow for others strengthens and ennobles human nature." This is a distinction worth remembering, particularly in times of distress. Whenever we feel life has been hard on us, instead of going off to our bedroom and locking the door, that is the ideal time for turning our grief outward and putting it to work as compassion for the sorrows of others. After all, everyone faces misfortunes in life—now and again, severe ones. If, in the midst of our own troubles, we can go to a grieving neighbor or to someone sick and offer help, we will find that while we are lifting their spirits, we are lifting our own as well. This is a perfect recipe both for nipping depression in the bud and for spreading consolation.

To be understood as to understand

When I first took to meditation, my attitude toward my students underwent a substantial change. You know, when you have been talking in class for five days running about Wordsworth's view of nature and on Friday you ask one or two simple questions and can get no satisfactory answer, it is natural to feel a bit exasperated. "Why can't they follow?" I used to ask myself "Or, if they cannot follow, why can they not at least read through the text at home so they can answer simple questions?"

Gradually, however, I began to develop a more compassionate attitude. It struck me forcefully that words like Saint Francis's were meant not only to be repeated in meditation but to be applied, even in mundane situations on a university campus. I began to understand, for example, that it was unreasonable to expect a good performance from a student who had an irresistible tendency to daydream and procrastinate. With that insight, my exasperation evaporated. I saw such problems now from my students' perspective, and instead of wishing they were different, my attention went to getting to know those students and helping them learn better habits. Teaching became a matter of not merely conveying knowledge, but of showing how to live.

Understanding is the first thing to jump out the window when two emotionally involved people get into a quarrel. "He just does not understand me!" is a grumble that frequently reaches my ears. Saint Francis, I suspect, would reply, "What does it matter? The real question is, do you understand him? Have you tried to understand his point of view?" The honest answer would usually be no. Strong emotions plug up our ears like those foam earplugs which expand into the opening of your ear to prevent even a single stray wave of sound from getting through.

I have yet to hear of anyone who did not understand his or her own side of a quarrel in minute detail. "See, my hay fever is acting up now because my prescription ran out, and I had this terrific headache from our youngest son yelling at me. So when my husband came into the kitchen and slammed the door for no reason, I just let him have it." Our private prosecuting attorney in the mind has built up an open-and-shut case. That is the problem: we shut the case a bit too soon. As any experienced judge knows, every case has two sides. Fairness demands that we give equal time to the defense, who is inside us too. The other side deserves the same hearing and the same benefit of the doubt that we give ourselves as a matter of course. This is detachment. Just as we are fallible and sometimes allow circumstances to get the better of us, so too the other person is fallible. If we remember this, quarrels can be settled amicably before they ever come before a jury.

To be loved as to love

Now we get down to the nitty-gritty of romance. Millions of people today voice the heartfelt complaint that they feel lonely and unloved. It is a serious condition. Here Saint Francis is say-ing, "I know the cause of the malady and I know the secret of its complete cure." No matter what the relationship may be, when you look on another person as someone who can give you love, you are really *faking* love. That is the simplest word for it. If you are interested in *making* love, in making it grow without end, try looking on that person as someone you can give your love to— someone to whom you can go on giving always.

Learning to love is like swimming against the current of a powerful river; most of our conditioning is in the other direc-tion. When the river by my village used to flood with the ad-vent of the monsoon rains we boys liked to try to swim across without being swept downstream by the current. To tell you the truth, I never succeeded. The only time I came close was the time someone told me there was a crocodile after me. But a few of my cousins were such powerful swimmers that they could fight the current and reach the other side exactly opposite from where they had set out. It is simply a question of developing your muscles: the more you use them, the stronger they get. Similarly, when you put the other person's welfare foremost every day, no matter how strong the opposing tide inside, you discover after a while that you can love a little more today than you did yesterday. Tomorrow you will be able to love a little more.

There is no end to love. It does not confine itself to just one person or one family. Most of us seem to feel that if Romeo, say, begins to care deeply for Juliet's nurse, his love for Juliet will somehow be diminished; Juliet should feel jealous. If he learns to extend his love to her brothers, the nurse should feel neglected too. There is no conflict. Romeo still loves Juliet and still cares for her nurse; it is just that he is coming to love everybody. He can be completely loyal to his sweetheart, Juliet, and completely loyal in all his other relationships as well. The beauty of this kind of love is that it never divides; it will bring Juliet, her nurse, and her brothers closer together than they ever were before.

EKNATH EASWARAN

For it is in giving that we receive

This is one of the most incredible paradoxes in life. We think, naturally enough, that if we go after what we want, we will probably get it; then we will be happy and secure. The mass media have latched onto this line of thinking and intone it like a litany: grab, grab, grab! Yet sooner or later the whole smorgasbord of things to get causes every sensitive person to ask, "If I go on grabbing and grabbing, at what point is it that I become secure and feel no more need to grab?" This question can lead to some far-reaching answers. Our needs are much too big to be satisfied with things, no matter how many we can manage to acquire. Often, it seems, the more we try to get, the more acutely we feel those needs.

We are used today to thinking in terms of presents—Father's Day presents, Mother's Day presents, birthday presents, Christmas presents. The great excitement at Christmas is looking in our stocking and opening gifts. Francis might ask, "Don't you want to find your stocking filled with good things every morning?" We *can*, every morning right after our meditation. But we cannot expect to find our stocking filled if we leave it hanging there full of stuff. There will be no room for the Lord to put anything in unless we empty ourselves every day by giving all we can in the way of kindness and loving help. Then every morning we will find ourselves full again—of love, of understanding, of forgiveness, of energy with which to carry these gifts to others. Saint Francis has been telling us in every line of this Prayer that this is the Lord's way of giving: the more we share what we have, the more he wants to give us.

Every day we can receive these gifts and every day we can share them, whether people are friendly to us or not. The more we share, the more we will win the love and respect of others—and the more we win their love and respect, the less our turmoil and troubles. Burdens will lie very lightly on us. Our deepest need is for the joy that comes with loving and being loved, with knowing we are of genuine use to others. For everybody who has problems or who wants to go forward steadily on the spiritual path, my recipe would be to do more for others and think less about yourself. Hang up an empty stocking and every day you will find your life filling more and more with joy.

It is in pardoning that we are pardoned

Late in his life Francis found it necessary to give over his place as head of the order to Brother Elias, who thereafter became very keen on improving the conduct of his Brothers. When Elias came to him with complaints and plans to penalize some of them, Francis gave him strong advice: "See to it that no Brother in the whole world, however he may have sinned, is permitted to go from you without forgiveness if he asks for it. And if he does not ask for forgiveness, then ask him if he does not want it. And even if he comes before your eyes a thousand times with sin, love him more than you do me, that you may draw him to the Lord; . . . for the healthy need no physician, but only those who suffer illness."

The forgiveness Francis is prescribing here is not a matter merely of saying "I forgive you; let bygones be bygones." No amount of talking can prevent the seed of resentment from taking hold in our heart. True forgiveness requires that we not only not take personally any harsh thing said or done to us, but that we make an all-out effort to understand the other person's situation. Then, even if we get angry for a few minutes and think, "That Mortimer!" we know it will soon turn to "Well, he comes from a discordant home, and nobody showed him how to object nicely." We know then that resentment really does not stand a chance. But Francis is zealous in his recommendation that we follow up this forgiving with concrete acts of love which can actually cure the impulse of the other person to say or do something harsh again.

It is in dying to self that we are born to eternal life

We all have deep within us an overwhelming desire to lose ourselves in love. In practical terms, this is what loving the Lord means. Saint Francis is reminding us again that the way to live in the presence of the Lord is to find that love which flows all the time, regardless of people's ups and downs, which brings together not only our own dear ones but all others as well. Finding this love requires a lot of labor and anguish, but it is this labor, which we accomplish by meditating and incorporating the other spiritual disciplines into our daily life, that opens the floodgates of love.

Loving the Lord has the miraculous power to change us. We all know how, when a young man feels drawn to a young lady, his personal appearance improves overnight, his language becomes more refined, his taste in reading and entertainment takes on a softer, more romantic bent. In just the same way, when we start to get intimations of what pleases the Lord our personality begins to change. We make more of an effort to be patient with people, and even if anger comes up, it has less sting. We actually start to sympathize with the difficulties others are facing. This is an inescapable transformation.

If you ask a spiritual figure how he can find joy in effacing himself, he will tell you, "Otherwise, I do not stand a chance; my Lord will not even look at me. He will say, 'Who wants this angry grouch around?' This gives us all the determination we need to empty ourselves. And when we succeed even a little, we feel ourselves moving that much closer to Him." They do tell us it can be very distressing at times, but the joy we find in this growing love will give us motivation to face distress with equanimity.

In time, we begin to enrich our life with concern for everybody, with giving our time and our energy to helping solve the problems that people around us are facing. By directing our attention to others' welfare, we make our own life fuller and more beautiful. This is the source of the spiritual figure's incredibly selfless, undemanding love which seems to us so uncanny. It was what Saint Bernard was hinting at when he gave this explanation: "I love because I love; I love in order that I may love." *When I do not love*, he is trying to tell us, *I am parted from my Lord; and that I cannot bear.*

IX

Alive to Love

by Vimala Thakar

Living that moves easily from silence to action to silence is meditation. There are many unfortunate misunderstandings about meditation. Many associate it with a life of contemplation, retreat, of donning special costumes and being very remote from the cries of human misery. In true meditation, there is the presence of wholeness, the awareness of totality in every breath, every moment, every movement of relationship. Totality, wholeness, oneness is ever present in meditation. Even though we may work in many fields of human activity, be involved in relationships, meet the needs of daily living, the wholeness remains. All of living has the perfume of wholeness, the tender concern, the passion of commitment, the vitality of being fully alive.

Meditation is a new dimension of life and consciousness for which the human race is groping all over the world. Explorations that are going on in the various countries, in different ways are creating currents which converge on only one point: transcending the mental, the psychological structure. We are eager to grow, to leave behind the worn-out mind, so that the vast immensity that lies behind the visible and invisible is exposed to awareness. And perhaps the fusion of the individual psyche with that immensity and infinity of life, may bring about an exponential change in the human race.

Meditation gives the passion for total revolution. Living on the level of the intellect, the mind, we lack the scope, the vital energy to make total revolution possible. We waste too much energy on petty disputes, ugly concerns about power and possession. Meditation creates energy, vitality, is not limited in scope, is not damaged by petty motives.

Living in meditation, compassion and love are facts, realities, not the romantic illusions or trivial hypocrisies they have become for most of us. In meditation defenses of the ego structure melt, then compassion and love which are realities in the cosmos but usually ignored, flow causelessly, choicelessly, abundantly.

The purity of the essence of life, the unconditioned isness, radiates in love and compassion. The radiance of love and compassion is ever present but we obscure the brilliance with our gross insensitivity.

Unfortunately, we have commercialized love, made it an object of entertainment in innumerable varieties of themes, almost beyond repair. The sanctity of love, and of beautiful mysteries of life cannot be marred, but the use of the word love in modern societies is often pathetic. There is energy in love and we exploit that energy by making love into currency, into an item of trade, buying security with love, bartering domination, agreement to be dominated, taking people into servitude in the name of love. And we reduce love to fulfillment of sensual pleasure, a petty, repetitive pleasure to soothe the sting of loneliness, insecurity, lack of deep fulfillment.

The Full Potential of Love

Love is obviously not all that; it's what is possible when all this silly business comes to an end, when all the ego manipulations are transcended, when the artificial boundaries of defense structures are dismantled, when there is no more motive to get something out of love.

Love is complete relaxation in wholeness, in oneness. There is no desire, no motive to push and pull at another's life, to force a person into something he or she is not out of our own images.

Love and faith are intricately intertwined. Without faith, relaxation will not be complete; there will always be the tension of not being at peace with the universe. And when there is tension love does not flower. Tension results in subtle violence against oneself and against others.

Love is sharing the earth, the joys, the sorrows, the beauty, the ugliness, in easy communion without trying to manipulate others in any way at all. There is respect for, and faith in, the innate intelligence of other's lives.

This is not to say that we are indifferent, uncaring, that we are not responsive as parents, children, friends to the sincere needs of loved ones, but in being responsive, we do not dominate, bind the other person in a net of psychological attachments. We do not use the force of personality charisma to bind others to us, to damage the freedom of another person in any way.

Love is responsive, but is light, free, without hooks to ensnare. Because it does not move from the ego, but is centerless, selfless, it does not have the motive to acquire sensual pleasure, to enhance self-image, to collect allies to be used in games of power.

The beauty, the mystery of love is that it is not of the ego, is not controlled by the conditioning, is not simply a desire for sensual pleasure. Because it is not conditioned, the touch of love, egoless love, heals our lives.

In the affluent countries, the emphasis on human-made structures and material goods, the homage that is given to mastery of the intellect, the depersonalization of the economic structures, the dependence on machines in almost all aspects of living has practically driven love out. Well-fed people are starved for affection, the milk of human kindness. And yet the developing countries, are racing to emulate the model of the west, to be dominated by science and technology, to collect a nauseating variety of consumer goods.

Love is essential if there is to be any quality to our lives, individually and collectively. If we are not to be barbarians, plundering and looting one another, then love must flourish everywhere.

New Motivation

Love provides a new motivation for collective living, a new motivation for transforming socioeconomic, political structures and systems. The full potential of love for collective living, for revolution has not been realized. We have had the negative examples of violence, power, struggle, conflict. Is it not time to unleash the positive light of love and let its warmth flood the land in healing radiance?

What is required is that as committed human beings, we have the fearlessness to set ourselves free of inner bondage, to go beyond the confines of the ego, and the motives of ego-centered living, to live in the wholeness of action and non-action, silence and sound, to open up to faith and the relaxation of love. If we hold on to bondage in any way at all, we are denying the freedom of love to ourselves and humanity.

We have moved very far away from love in our collective lives, dangerously near self-destruction, close to starvation. Perhaps we have the wisdom now, the awareness that love is as essential to human beings as the air we breath, the water we drink, the food we eat. Love is the beauty, the delicate mystery, the soul of life, the radiant unspoiled purity that brings spontaneous joy, songs of ecstasy, poems, paintings, dance, dramas to celebrate its indescribable, never-to-be-fully captured bliss of being.

Can we bring love into the market places, into the homes, the schools, the places of business and transform them completely? You may call it a utopian challenge, but it is the only one that will make a significant difference, that is fully worthy of the potential of whole human beings.

PART THREE

Love and Wisdom

Sometimes I know that I am everything,
and I call that love.
Sometimes I know that I am nothing,
and I call that wisdom.
Between love and wisdom my life continually flows.

Nisargadatta Maharaj

There came a voice resonant with divinity. It said: "Oh, there is a love which fears nothing, which is greater than life and greater than death. I am that Love. There is a Love which knows no limit, which is everywhere, which is in the presence of death, and which is all-tender even in the terrible. I am that Love.

There is a Love which is unutterably Sweet, which welcomes all pain, which welcomes all fear, which drives away all sadness, which is wheresoever thou dost search for it. I am that Love. Oh, I am the very Essence of that love. And, O, my own Self, I, that Love, am thine own Self. My nature is love, I am Love itself.

F. J. Alexander
In the Hour of Meditation

X

The Unity of Wisdom and Love

by Swami Amar Jyoti

The climax of wisdom, salvation and highest philosophy is Supreme Realization, Vedantic Realization. *Sarvam Kalvidam Brahman*—Everything is *Brahman*. Everything is Truth, Reality, Spirit, Light. Thou *art* That. You and the cosmos are One. Your Spirit, your God, your *being*—all are One. Two ways bifurcate from this Vedantic Realization. One is transcendental, in which you are merged into Oneness with the Cosmos; where nothing has ever happened and nothing has been created. In that pervadedness, that liberation, ultimate Transcendence, questions regarding creation do not exist. The second way proceeds with the Immanent manifesting through creation.

Any manifestation *has* to have a Creator, the Lord and Engineer. We cannot separate God from the Absolute. God has existence—without Him or Her (or both) we would have no existence. Nothing in creation can have form without being created by one with form. Those who believe in the creation and do not believe in God the Creator will reach nowhere; they end only in frustration. When you reach Transcendence, the all-pervadedness of the Divine, the question of worship does not arise. You have merged with That. But as soon as you come to the world, yourself, your life, if you ignore or deny the Lord, you will remain dissatisfied. That is the import behind the two ways of Vedanta.

Shankaracharya was the first to clarify this misconception. He was one of the greatest Vedantists ever born, and yet in his last years was known for going to temples, worshiping the deities and singing hymns of glory to the Lord and Mother Divine. Many of his adherents, who really wanted Vedantic Realization—which is certainly the acme of all philosophies—were amazed and confused by this. How can this highest philosopher of Vedanta engage in such non-Vedantic activity, they wondered. They asked him, "How is it, sir, that such a great teacher as yourself, is now mixing this dualistic, *bhakti* (devotion) path with non-dualistic Absolute Transcendence?" He replied to them, "That is what Vedanta has taught me—how to worship the Lord."

> When true perception dawns, you will understand
> how the Absolute correlates with relativity,
> how *Brahman* correlates with the creation,
> how Spirit correlates with our lives.

The famous sage, Vedavyas, after completing the immortal scriptures, the Vedas, Upanishads, and epics—the highest wisdom existing on this earth—still felt unsatisfied. He prayed to the Lord, asking why, and Narada, the celestial messenger of Lord Narayan, appeared before him. (Vedavyas was no ordinary person, he was a great sage, one of the seven immortal sages according to Hindu tradition.) Narada told him, "You have written the immortal wisdom in which everything is contained, but you forgot one thing. You have written about all the paths: yoga, devotion, wisdom, *raja yoga*, self-inquiry, *tantra*, and many others, but you have failed to glorify the Lord. You believe in all the forms within creation—how is it that you have not sung the praise of the Lord who created all this? You are ignoring the very thread that connects all creation." Vedavyas understood, and, after Narada departed, meditated upon the Lord; afterwards, he wrote the famous *Srimad Bhagavatam*, the Gospel of Sri Krishna.

Many distinguish between the Absolute and God with form; they think to divide the Divine with their cold-blooded intellectualism. Often when you are lost in manifestation, in fulfilling selfish desires, you get engrossed in pleasantries and forget the Power behind it all. Some may think, "Oh, I can do without God." For how long? Without this integral connection, we will not be able to reconcile Spirit and life, the Absolute and relative creation. Those who want to grab everything to themselves, without thinking *who* gives, are bound to be frustrated.

The great Indian saint and Vedantist, Gauranga Chaitanya Mahaprabhu, like Shankaracharya and other revered realized souls, climaxed with the uttering of only two and a half letters [in Sanskrit]: *prema*—love. If anyone came to discuss scriptures or theology with him, he would accept defeat right away. Without hesitation, he would bow down to them and say: "Forgive me, sir, I already accept defeat. After studying volumes of books, I have learned only this one word: love. What can I discuss?" This is the pinnacle of Vedantic wisdom—attaining that full, pervading enlightenment, the essential unity of the cosmos, where there is only Transcendence and the Absolute.

Without love, creation would have no meaning—it wouldn't exist. But see the tragedy: although love is the very root cause of creation, life has become devoid of love because of ego. The very purpose of creation has been sacrificed! On one hand, consciousness of the Absolute is lost, and then we also lose love of the Lord. How much satisfaction can ego give us? This is why we have degraded.

Relative and Absolute Love

> The prophets, sages, and realized souls have been
> the greatest lovers, because they really know
> what love means. It is the unity between you
> and your Lord, between you and your Source.

There are two kinds of love: relative and absolute, also called unconditional. Relative love has its demands, obligations, duties, and commitments. It has the wish of reciprocation and the imposition or slavery of expectations. It is still called love, but such limited love will never be satisfying because of its dualistic nature. It remains under the sway of ego. Nevertheless, everyone hankers after love. Vedavyas divided relative love in four categories which cover all situations in life. We love: because someone likes or is attracted to us; because they are from our home or village or town; because they share the same nationality or religion or because we think alike or have many things in common; because they fulfill my desires or expectations. Conversely, these four categories reveal why you hate or dislike a person, or are prejudiced or jealous or repelled by anyone. Either he or she is not like you, or not fulfilling your expectations, or not from your culture, or their nature is not like yours.

Unconditional love is attained after wisdom is born. It transcends relative love and is not conditioned by where you live, whether you like someone or not, or whether your nature is different than theirs. Then you love regardless of whether someone is a sinner or virtuous, low or high, woman or man; you love all—animals, plants, the elements, the stars. You love for no reason, and your love is constant and satisfying. That is the Lord's Love, *agape*. Such love cannot come through intellectual gymnastics, but only after you are really immersed in wisdom. This is the divine love of Radha and Krishna, who are the perfect embodiment of love and wisdom. When that love awakens, there is nothing you can do but love. You can love your enemy, someone extremely opposite from yourself. This Vedantic Realization brings you to the Lord more directly, more purely, more unconditionally than you could have ever reached through the relative plane of love and devotion.

Wisdom and love are not two separate things; one leads to the other. You miss wisdom because you are tied up in self-imposed considerations; you want or expect others to like you or to synchronize with your nature, and think by that, "my unity will be achieved." Selfishness, delusion, demands and expectations are why love remains unsatisfying, whereas unconditional love is always satisfying. It does not *seek* satisfaction.

We allow very insignificant things to shatter our peace of mind. We can't stand differences of opinion; we want everybody to be like us, and everybody wants us to be like him or her. Unconditional love is not seeking unity in the sense of uniformity, but amidst diversity. People may be good and bad, virtuous and sinners, high and low, rich and poor, healthy and diseased. The Vedas call it variety. Amidst the variety, like a thread running through, is the underlying unity. You are realizing the Lord, Ishwara, who is the Creator. Therefore we worship.

The Purpose of Meditation

> That true love, God's love, is what permeates everything.
> To realize this unconditional love, we need absolute wisdom.
> This is the purpose of meditation.

There are two paths to take: wisdom and devotion, *jñāna* and *bhakti*. *Jñāna* is the path of self-inquiry or intellect; *bhakti* is the path through the heart, the love of the Lord. Wisdom has been called the "father" and devotion the "mother," but they are inseparable. Wise men devoid of love and lovers without wisdom are both ignorant. Wisdom and love substantiate each other. The more wisdom, the more love; the more love, the more wisdom. If you find a lover who is a dullard, do not believe his/her love—it must be selfish gratification. True love awakens wisdom and opens a wise man's heart. Einstein said, "God is subtle, but He's not malicious." A loving person cannot be malicious.

The only way you really experience or give love is through achieving wisdom, through enlightenment, when you *know yourself.* Wisdom is simplicity, pure love for the Lord. The simple-hearted reach there. They are wise, they love—nobody else. Complex ones are frustrated and confused; they cannot love. Complexity and simplicity do not go together. You cannot be tricky and honest at the same time.

There is a way, the way of the initiates. There is a path that unites wisdom and love, and solves all the riddles of life. Psychology and counseling may help, but they cannot give the ultimate solution.

Finding the Root Connection

> The answer to life's challenges,
> the successes and failures, cannot be
> outside us; sufferings, wants and losses
> must all be connected to us.
> We have to find this root connection.

When we come to the real marriage of intellect and heart, we will understand the relationship of the Absolute and God with form and ourselves. There are three factors here: the Transcendental, which is called absolute nondualistic, non-relative, the pervading sense, Reality; the Lord with form, God, Ishwara, the Creator; and souls such as you and I. And yet these are not actually three, they are One. Where you miss this connection, the trouble begins, and any kind of patchwork won't work. In this Oneness, all incarnations take place. It reveals the secret of life on earth and on other planets, how it is created and sustained through *māyā* and illusion.

If we worship the Lord, we will do His will. If we worship Him and do our own will, we remain unconscious. This reconciliation between the Absolute and the creation may be the answer for the New Age. Many "new agers" have seemingly brushed God away, as if they do not need Him because they are so progressed. We may have progressed, but what are the results? Let the results speak for themselves.

Real Love

> When we truly understand God's working,
> we will come to real love, *anurāga*,
> and dedication to the Lord. We will feel
> His tangible existence, and it will bring
> tears to our eyes.

We are not talking about tears of joy, but tears of separation and pathos. We weep for Him because we have not *seen* Him. If we are impure and full of desires, greed and selfishness—spiritual materialism—how can we weep for God? To weep for God we need a pure heart, a simple heart. Do not ask the Lord to make you weep for Him. Why, then, shouldn't He make the stones weep? Do we wait for God's grace to weep for other things in life? How do we weep, automatically, over matters which concern us? If someone slaps us or insults us, or we are in pain or disease, or we sustain some kind of loss, don't we weep? Do you pray to the Lord to make you weep for material gain? Only when it comes to weeping for the Lord do we stand helpless!

Often what we term innocence under closer analysis proves to be not only stupidity but manipulation or cleverness. We have to scrutinize ourselves very carefully. Even if you pray to the Lord to make you weep for Him, at least let that prayer be *honest*. It might work. But we are afraid it might work, so we are not honest in that either. Underneath is the fear that if we really pray sincerely and He makes us truly weep, everything will melt and we will be vulnerable. We are afraid of being vulnerable to the Lord! This is the tragedy of modern man. What a great joy there is in being vulnerable to the Almighty!

Why this fear of vulnerability? It is epidemic nowadays. Children are not afraid of being vulnerable, but adults, with our so-called wisdom, our "consciousness," why do we fear being vulnerable to the Lord? Isn't that another form of faithlessness? Ego obstructs so much; there is no end to its games. We have to be simple like children to weep for the Lord, or we end up with trickiness. Let's be simple and honest, true lovers of the Lord. Let's make that the purpose of our lives.

> Love is an invincible magic.
> Not love as you and I may desire,
> but born out of wisdom.
> Where you really know.

Where one does not cancel out the other. You could differ with a person but still love them. You do not have to curse anyone; they will reap the results of their karma anyway. We don't have to have ill-feelings for anyone, just leave them alone. Be neutral, what we call detached. In that, you do not incur karmas, you just let others experience their own karmas. This is the way to reconcile love of the Lord with Wisdom and still maintain life. Within our own sphere of existence, the three-dimensional plane, we can still maintain the Divine Purpose of life; where we come to full satisfaction; where our relationships, way of living, intellect and heart are fully integrated; where body, vital sheath, emotions and thoughts are in unison with the Divine. If we understand this, not rejecting life but attaining to Life Divine, we will come to New Age Consciousness.

XI

Dropping the Illusions

by Anthony de Mello

If we really dropped illusions for what they can give us or deprive us of, we would be alert. The consequence of not doing this is terrifying and inescapable. We lose our capacity to love. If you wish to love, you must learn to see again. And if you wish to see, you must learn to give up your drug. It is as simple as that. Give up your dependency. Tear away the tentacles of society that have enveloped and suffocated your being. You must drop them. Externally, everything will go on as before, but though you will continue to be *in* the world, you will no longer be *of* it. In your heart, you will now be free at last, if utterly alone. Your dependence on your drug will die. You do not have to go to the desert; you are right in the middle of people; you are enjoying them immensely. But they no longer have the power to make you happy or miserable. That is what aloneness means. In this solitude your dependence dies. The capacity to love is born. One no longer sees others as means of satisfying one's addiction. Only someone who has attempted this knows the terrors of the process. It's like inviting yourself to die. It's like asking the poor drug addict to give up the only happiness he has ever known. How to replace it with the taste of bread and fruit and the clean taste of the morning air, the sweetness of the water of the mountain stream? While he is struggling with his withdrawal symptoms and the emptiness he experiences within himself now that his drug is gone, nothing can fill the emptiness except his drug. Can you imagine a life in which you refuse to enjoy or take pleasure in a single word of appreciation or to rest your head on anyone's shoulder for support? Think of a life in which you depend on no one emotionally, so that no one has the power to make you happy or miserable anymore. You refuse to *need* any particular person or to be special to anyone or to call anyone your own. The birds of the air have their nests and the foxes their holes, but you will have nowhere to rest your head in your journey through life. If you ever get to this state, you will at last know what it means to see with a vision that is clear and unclouded by fear or desire. Every word there is measured. *To see at last with a vision that is clear and unclouded by fear or desire.* You will know what it means to love. But to come to the land of love, you must pass through the pains of death, for to love persons means to die to the need for persons, and to be utterly alone.

Ceaseless Awareness

How would you ever get there? By a ceaseless awareness, by the infinite patience and compassion you would have for a drug addict. By developing a taste for the good things in life to counter the craving for your drug. What good things? The love of work which you enjoy doing for the love of itself; the love of laughter and intimacy with people to whom you do not cling and on whom you do not depend emotionally but whose company you enjoy. It will also help if you take on activities that you can do with your *whole being*, activities that you so love to do that while you're engaged in them, success, recognition, and approval simply do not mean a thing to you. It will help, too, if you return to nature. Send the crowds away, go up to the mountains, and silently commune with trees and flowers and animals and birds, with sea and clouds and sky and stars. I've told you what a spiritual exercise it is to gaze at things, to be aware of things around you. Hopefully, the words will drop, the concepts will drop, and you will see, you will make contact with reality. That is the cure for loneliness. Generally, we seek to cure our loneliness through emotional dependence on people, through gregariousness and noise. That is no cure. Get back to things, get back to nature, go up in the mountains. Then you will know that your heart has brought you to the vast desert of solitude, there is no one there at your side, absolutely no one.

At first this will seem unbearable. But it is only because you are unaccustomed to aloneness. If you manage to stay there for a while, the desert will suddenly blossom into love. Your heart will burst into song. And it will be springtime forever; the drug will be out; you're free. Then you will understand what freedom is, what love is, what happiness is, what reality is, what truth is, what God is. You will see, you will know beyond concepts and conditioning, addictions and attachments. Does that make sense?

Let me end this with a lovely story. There was a man who invented the art of making fire. He took his tools and went to a tribe in the north, where it was very cold, bitterly cold. He taught the people there to make fire. The people were very interested. He showed them the uses to which they could put fire—they could cook, could keep themselves warm, and so on. They were so grateful that they had learned the art of making fire. But before they could express their gratitude to the man, he disappeared. He wasn't concerned with getting their recognition or gratitude; he was concerned about their well-being. He went to another tribe, where he again began to show them the value of his invention. People were interested there, too, a bit too interested for the peace of mind of their priests, who began to notice that this man was drawing crowds and they were losing their popularity. So they decided to do away with him. They poisoned him, crucified him, put it any way you like. But they were afraid now that the people might turn against them, so they were very wise, even wily. Do you know what they did? They had a portrait of the man made and mounted it on the main altar of the temple. The instruments for making fire were placed in front of the portrait, and the people were taught to revere the portrait and to pay reverence to the instruments of fire, which they dutifully did for centuries. The veneration and the worship went on, but there was no fire.

Where's the fire? Where's the love? Where's the drug uprooted from your system? Where's the freedom? This is what spirituality is all about. Tragically, we tend to lose sight of this, don't we? This is what Jesus Christ is all about. But we overemphasized the "Lord, Lord," didn't we? Where's the fire? And if worship isn't leading to fire, if adoration isn't leading to love, if the liturgy isn't leading to a clearer perception of reality, if God isn't leading to life, of what use is religion except to create more division, more fanaticism, more antagonism? It is not from lack of religion in the ordinary sense of the word that the world is suffering, it is from lack of love, lack of awareness. And love is generated through awareness and through no other way, no other way. Understand the obstructions you are putting in the way of love, freedom, and happiness and they will drop. Turn on the light of awareness and the darkness will disappear. Happiness is not something you acquire; love is not something you produce; love is not something that you have; love is something that *has* you. You do not have the wind, the stars, and the rain. You don't possess these things; you surrender to them. And surrender occurs when you are aware of your illusions, when you are aware of your addictions, when you are aware of your desires and fears.

Self-Understanding

As I told you earlier, first, psychological insight is a great help, not analysis, however; analysis is paralysis. Insight is not necessarily analysis. One of your great American therapists put it very well: "It's the 'Aha' experience that counts." Merely analyzing gives no help; it just gives information. But if you could produce the "Aha" experience, that's insight. That is change.

Second, the understanding of your addiction is important. You need time. Alas, so much time that is given to worship and singing praise and singing songs could so fruitfully be employed in self-understanding. Community is not produced by joint liturgical celebrations. You know deep down in your heart, and so do I, that such celebrations only serve to paper over differences. Community is created by understanding the blocks that we put in the way of community, by understanding the conflicts that arise from our fears and our desires. At that point community arises. We must always beware of making worship just another distraction from the important business of living. And living doesn't mean working in government, or being a big businessman, or performing great acts of charity. That isn't living. Living is to have dropped all the impediments and to live in the present moment with freshness. "The birds of the air. . . they neither toil nor spin,"—that is living. I began by saying that people are asleep, dead. Dead people running governments, dead people running big business, dead people educating others; come alive! Worship must help this, or else it's useless. And increasingly—you know this and so do I—we're losing the youth everywhere. They hate us; they're not interested in having more fears and more guilt laid on them. They're not interested in more sermons and exhortations. But they are interested in learning about love. How can I be happy? How can I live? How can I taste the marvelous things that the mystics speak of? So that's the second thing—understanding.

Third, don't identify. Somebody asked me as I was coming here today, "Do you ever feel low?" Boy, do I feel low every now and then. I get my attacks. But they don't last, they really don't. What do I do?

First step: I don't identify. Here comes a low feeling. Instead of getting tense about it, instead of getting irritated with myself about it, I understand I'm feeling depressed, disappointed, or whatever.

Second step: I admit the feeling is in me, not in the other person, that is, in the person who didn't write me a letter, not in the exterior world; it's in me. Because as long as I think it's outside me, I feel justified in holding on to my feelings. I can't say everybody would feel this way; in fact, only idiotic people would feel this way, only sleeping people.

Third step: I don't identify with the feeling. "I" is not that feeling. "I" am not lonely, "I" am not depressed, "I" am not disappointed. Disappointment is *there*, one watches it. You'd be amazed how quickly it glides away. Anything you're aware of keeps changing; clouds keep moving. As you do this, you also get all kinds of insights into why clouds were coming in the first place.

XII

The Spirit of Unconditional Love

by Ralph Waldo Trine

The moment we recognize ourselves as one with the spirit of infinite love we become so filled with love that we see only the good in all. And when we realize that we are all one with this infinite Spirit, then we realize that in a sense we are all one with each other. When we come into a recognition of this fact, we can then do no harm to any one, to any thing. We find that we are all members of the one great body, and that no portion of the body can be harmed without all the other portions suffering thereby.

When we fully realize the great fact of the oneness of all life—that all are partakers from this one infinite Source, and so that the same life is the life in each individual, then prejudices go and hatreds cease. Love grows and reigns supreme. Then, wherever we go, whenever we come in contact with our fellow human beings, we are able to recognize the God within. We thus look only for the good, and we find it. It always pays.

There is a deep scientific fact underlying the great truth, "He that takes the sword shall perish by the sword." The moment we come into a realization of the subtle powers of the thought forces, we can quickly see that the moment we entertain any thoughts of hatred toward another, he gets the effects of these diabolical forces that go out from us, and has the same thoughts of hatred aroused in him, which in turn return to the sender. Then when we understand the effects of the passion, hatred or anger even upon the physical body, we can see how detrimental, how expensive this is. The same is true in regard to all kindred thoughts or passions, envy, criticism, jealousy, scorn. In the ultimate we shall find that in entertaining feelings of this nature toward another, we always suffer far more than the one toward whom we entertain them.

And then when we fully realize the fact that selfishness is at the root of all error, sin, and crime, and that ignorance is the basis of all selfishness, with what charity we come to look upon the acts of all. It is the ignorant man who seeks his own ends at the expense of the greater whole. It is the ignorant man, therefore, who is the selfish man. The truly wise man is never selfish. He is a seer, and recognizes the fact that he, a single member of the one great body, is benefited in just the degree that the entire body is benefited, and so he seeks nothing for himself that he would not equally seek for all mankind.

If selfishness is at the bottom of all error, sin, and crime, and ignorance is the basis of all selfishness, then when we see a manifestation of either of these qualities, if we are true to the highest within us, we will look for and will seek to call forth the good in each individual with whom we come in contact. When God speaks to God, then God responds, and shows forth as God. But when devil speaks to devil, then devil responds, and the devil is always to pay.

I sometimes hear a person say, "I don't see any good in him." No? Then you are no seer. Look deeper and you will find the very God in every human soul. But remember it takes a God to recognize a God. Christ always spoke to the highest, the truest, and the best in men. He knew and he recognized the God in each because he had first realized it in himself. He ate with publicans and sinners. Abominable, the Scribes and Pharisees said. They were so wrapped up in their own conceits, their own self-centeredness, in their own ignorance, that they had never found the God in themselves, and so they never dreamed that it was the real life of even publicans and sinners.

In the degree that we hold a person in the thought of evil or of error, do we suggest evil and error to him. In the degree that he is sensitively organized or not well individualized and so subject to the suggestions of the thought forces from others, will he be influenced; and so in this way we may be sharers in the very evil doing in which we hold another in thought. In the same way when we hold a person in the thoughts of the higher, the good, and the true, righteousness, goodness, and truth are suggested to him, and thus we have a most beneficial influence on his life and conduct. If our hearts go out in love to all with whom we come in contact, we inspire love, and the same ennobling and warming influences of love always return to us from those in whom we inspire them. There is a deep scientific principle underlying the precept: If you would have all the world love you, you must first love all the world.

The Power of Love

In the degree that we love will we be loved. Thoughts are forces. Each creates of its kind. Each comes back laden with the effect that corresponds to itself and of which it is the cause.

> Then let your secret thoughts be fair
> They have a vital part, and share
> In shaping words and molding fate
> God's system is so intricate.

I know of no better practice than that of a friend who continually holds himself in an attitude of mind that he continually sends out his love in the form of the thoughts: "Dear everybody, I love you." And when we realize the fact that a thought invariably produces its effect before it returns, or before it ceases, we can see how he is continually breathing out a blessing not only upon all with whom he comes in contact, but upon all the world. These same thoughts of love, moreover, tokened in various ways, are continually coming to him from all quarters.

Even animals feel the effects of these forces. Some animals are much more sensitively organized than many people are, and consequently they get the effects of our thoughts, our mental states, and emotions much more readily than many people do. Therefore whenever we meet an animal we can do it good by sending out to it these thoughts of love. It will feel the effects whether we simply entertain or whether we voice them. And it is often interesting to note how quickly it responds, and how readily it gives evidence of its appreciation of this love and consideration on our part.

What a privilege and how enjoyable it would be to live and walk in a world where we meet only Gods. In such a world you can live. In such a world I can live. For in the degree that we come into this higher realization do we see only the God in each human soul, and when we are thus able to see Him in every one we meet, we then live in such a world.

And when we thus recognize the God in every one, by this recognition we help to call it forth ever more and more. What a privilege—this privilege of yours, this privilege of mine! That hypocritical judging of another is something then with which we can have nothing to do; for we have the power of looking beyond the evolving, changing, error-making self, and seeing the real, the changeless, the eternal Self which by and by will show forth in the full beauty of holiness. We are then large enough also to realize the fact that when we condemn another, by that very act we condemn ourselves.

This realization so fills us with love that we continually overflow with it, and all with whom we come in contact feel its warming and life-giving power. These in turn send back the same feelings of love to us, and so we continually attract love from all quarters. Tell me how much one loves and I will tell you how much he has seen of God. Tell me how much he loves and I will tell you how much he lives with God. Tell me how much he loves and I will tell you how far into the Kingdom of Heaven, the kingdom of harmony, he has entered, for "love is the fulfilling of the law." . . .

The Divine Method

The truly wise man or woman will recognize no one as an enemy. Occasionally we hear the expression, "Never mind; I will get even with him." Will you? And how will you do it? You can do it in one of two ways. You can, as you have in mind, deal with him as he deals, or apparently deals with you—pay him, as we say, in his own coin. If you do this you will get even with him by sinking yourself to his level, and both of you will suffer by it. Or, you can show yourself the larger, you can send him love for hatred, kindness for ill-treatment, and so get even with him by raising him to the higher level. But remember that you can never help another without by that very act helping yourself; and if forgetful of self, then in most all cases the value to you is greater than the service you render another. If you are ready to treat him as he treats you, then you show clearly that there is in you that which draws the hatred and ill-treatment to you; you deserve what you are getting and should not complain, nor would you complain if you were wise. By following the other course you most effectually accomplish your purpose, you gain a victory for yourself, and at the same time you do a great service for him, for which it is evident he stands greatly in need.

Thus you become his savior. He in turn may become the savior of other error-making, and consequently care-encumbered men and women. Many times the struggles are greater than we can ever know. We need more gentleness and sympathy and compassion in our common human life. Then we will neither blame nor condemn. Instead of blaming or condemning we will sympathize, and all the more we will:

> Comfort one another,
> For the way is often dreary,
> And the feet are often weary,

And the heart is very sad.
There is a heavy burden bearing,
When it seems that none are caring,
And we half forget that ever we were glad.

Comfort one another
With the handclasp close and tender,
With the sweetness love can render,
And the looks of friendly eyes.
Do not wait with grace unspoken,
While life's daily beat is broken—
Gentle speech is oft like manna from the skies.

When we come fully to realize the great fact that all evil and error and sin with all their consequent sufferings come through ignorance, then wherever we see a manifestation of these in whatever form, if our hearts are right, we will have compassion, sympathy and compassion for the one in whom we see them. Compassion will then change itself into love, and love will manifest itself in kindly service. Such is the divine method. And so instead of aiding in trampling and keeping a weaker one down, we will hold him up until he can stand alone and become the master. But all life-growth is from within out, and one becomes a true master in the degree that the knowledge of the divinity of his own nature dawns upon his inner consciousness and so brings him to a knowledge of the higher laws; and in no way can we so effectually hasten this dawning in the inner consciousness of another, as by showing forth the divinity within ourselves simply by the way we live.

By example and not by precept. By living, not by preaching. By doing, not by professing. By living the life, not by dogmatizing as to how it should be lived. There is no contagion equal to the contagion of life. Whatever we sow, that shall we also reap, and each thing sown produces of its kind. We can kill not only by doing another bodily injury directly, but we can and we do kill by every antagonistic thought. Not only do we thus kill, but while we kill we commit suicide. Many a man has been made sick by having the ill thoughts of a number of people centered upon him; some have been actually killed. Put hatred into the world and we make it a literal hell. Put love into the world and heaven with all its beauties and glories becomes a reality.

Not to love is not to live, or it is to live a living death. The life that goes out in love to all is the life that is full, and rich, and continually expanding in beauty and in power. Such is the life that becomes ever more inclusive, and hence larger in its scope and influence. The larger the man and the woman the more inclusive they are in their love and their friendships. The smaller the man and the woman, the more dwarfed and dwindling their natures, the more they pride themselves upon their "exclusiveness." Any one—a fool or an idiot—can be exclusive. It comes easy. It takes and it signifies a large nature to be universal, to be inclusive. Only the man or the woman of a small, personal, self-centered, self-seeking nature is exclusive. The man or the woman of a large, royal, unself-centered nature never is. The small nature is the one that continually strives for effect. The larger nature never does. The one goes here and there in order to gain recognition, in order to attach himself to the world. The other stays at home and draws the world *to him*. The one loves merely himself. The other loves all the world; but in his larger love for all the world he finds himself included.

In Tune with the Infinite

Verily, then, the more one loves the nearer he approaches to God, for God is the spirit of infinite love. And when we come into the realization of our oneness with this Infinite Spirit, then divine love so fills us that, enriching and enrapturing our own lives, from them it flows out to enrich the life of all the world.

In coming into the realization of our oneness with the infinite Life, we are brought at once into right relations with our fellowmen. We are brought into harmony with the great law, that we find our own lives in losing them in the service of others. We are brought to a knowledge of the fact that all life is one, and so that we are all parts of the one great whole. We then realize that we cannot do for another without at the same time doing for ourselves. We also realize that we cannot do harm to another without by that very act doing harm to ourselves. We realize that the man who lives to himself alone lives a little, dwarfed, and stunted life, because he has no part in this larger life of humanity. But the one who in service loses his own life in this larger life, has his own life increased and enriched a thousand or a million fold, and every joy, every happiness, everything of value coming to each member of this greater whole comes as such to him, for he has a part in the life of each and all.

And here let a word be said in regard to true service. Peter and John were one day going up to the temple, and as they were entering the gate they were met by a poor cripple who asked them for alms. Instead of giving him something to supply the day's needs and then leaving him in the same dependent condition for the morrow and the morrow, Peter did him a real service, and a real service for all mankind by saying, silver and gold have I none, but such as I have I give unto thee. *And then he made him whole.* He thus brought him into the condition where he could help himself. In other words, the greatest service we can do for another is to help him to help himself. To help him directly might be weakening, though not necessarily. It depends entirely upon the circumstances. But to help one to help himself is never weakening, but always encouraging and strengthening, because it leads him to a larger and stronger life.

There is no better way to help one to help himself than to bring him to a knowledge of himself. There is no better way to bring one to a knowledge of himself than to lead him to a knowledge of the powers that are lying dormant within his own soul.

There is nothing that will enable him to come more readily or more completely into an awakened knowledge of the powers that are lying dormant within his own soul, than to bring him into the conscious, vital realization of his oneness with the infinite Life and power, so that he may open himself to it in order that it may work and manifest through him.

We will find that these same great truths lie at the very bottom of the solution of our social situation; and we will also find that we will never have a full and permanent solution of it until they are fully recognized and built upon.

XIII

Greeting the Day with Love

by Og Mandino

[*The following article is taken from Og Mandino's inspirational best-seller* "The Greatest Salesman in the World."]

I will greet this day with love in my heart.

For this is the greatest secret of success in all ventures. Muscle can split a shield and even destroy life but only the unseen power of love can open the hearts of men and until I master this art I will remain no more than a peddler in the market place. I will make love my greatest weapon and none on whom I call can defend against its force.

My reasoning they may counter; my speech they may distrust; my apparel they may disapprove; my face they may reject; and even my bargains may cause them suspicion; yet my love will melt all hearts liken to the sun whose rays soften the coldest clay.

I will greet this day with love in my heart.

And how will I do this? Henceforth will I look on all things with love and I will be born again. I will love the sun for it warms my bones; yet I will love the rain for it cleanses my spirit. I will love the light for it shows me the way; yet I will love the darkness for it shows me the stars. I will welcome happiness for it enlarges my heart; yet I will endure sadness for it opens my soul. I will acknowledge rewards for they are my due; yet I will welcome obstacles for they are my challenge.

I will greet this day with love in my heart.

And how will I speak? I will laud mine enemies and they will become friends; I will encourage my friends and they will become brothers. Always will I dig for reasons to applaud; never will I scratch for excuses to gossip. When I am tempted to criticize I will bite on my tongue; when I am moved to praise I will shout from the roofs.

Is it not so that birds, the wind, the sea and all nature speaks with the music of praise for their creator? Cannot I speak with the same music to his children? Henceforth will I remember this secret and it will change my life.

I will greet this day with love in my heart.

And how will I act? I will love all manners of men for each has qualities to be admired even though they be hidden. With love I will tear down the wall of suspicion and hate which they have built round their hearts and in its place will I build bridges so that my love may enter their souls.

I will love the ambitious for they can inspire me! I will love the failures for they can teach me. I will love the kings for they are but human; I will love the meek for they are divine. I will love the rich for they are yet lonely; I will love the poor for they are so many. I will love the young for the faith they hold; I will love the old for the wisdom they share. I will love the beautiful for their eyes of sadness; I will love the ugly for their souls of peace.

Love Alone

I will greet this day with love in my heart.

But how will I react to the actions of others? With love. For just as love is my weapon to open the hearts of men, love is also my shield, to repulse the arrows of hate and the spears of anger. Adversity and discouragement will beat against my new shield and become as the softest of rains. My shield will protect me in the marketplace and sustain me when I am alone. It will uplift me in moments of despair yet it will calm me in time of exultation. It will become stronger and more protective with use until one day I will cast it aside and walk unencumbered among all manners of men and, when I do, my name will be raised high on the pyramid of life.

I will greet this day with love in my heart.

And how will I confront each whom I meet? In only one way. In silence and to myself I will address him and say, "I love you." Though spoken in silence these words will shine in my eyes, unwrinkle my brow, bring a smile to my lips, and echo in my voice; and his heart will be opened. And who is there who will say nay to my goods when his heart feels my love?

I will greet this day with love in my heart.

And most of all I will love myself. For when I do I will zealously inspect all things which enter my body, my mind, my soul, and my heart. Never will I overindulge the requests of my flesh, rather I will cherish my body with cleanliness and moderation. Never will I allow my mind to be attracted to evil and despair, rather I will uplift it with the knowledge and wisdom of the ages. Never will I allow my soul to become complacent and satisfied, rather I will feed it with meditation and prayer. Never will I allow my heart to become small and bitter, rather I will share it and it will grow and warm the earth.

I will greet this day with love in my heart.

Henceforth will I love all mankind. From this moment all hate is let from my veins for I have not time to hate, only time to love. From this moment I take the first step required to become a man among men. With love I will increase my sales a hundred-fold and become a great salesman. If I have no other qualities I can succeed with love alone. Without it I will fail though I possess all the knowledge and skills of the world.

I will greet this day with love, and I will succeed.

Pronunciation of Sanskrit Letters

a	(b*u*t)	k	(*s*kate)	ḍ	⎰ no	m	(*m*uch)
ā	(m*o*m)	kh	(*K*ate)	ḍh	⎱ English	y	(*y*oung)
i	(*i*t)	g	(*g*ate)	ṇ	⎰ equiva-	r	(d*r*ama)
ī	(b*ee*t)	gh	(*g*awk)		⎱ lent	l	(*l*uck)
u	(s*u*ture)	ṅ	(*s*ing)	t	(*t*ell)	v	(*w*ile/*v*ile)
ū	(p*oo*l)	c	(*ch*unk)	th	(*t*ime)	ś	(*sh*ove)
ṛ	(*r*ig)	ch	(mat*ch*)	d	(*d*uck)	ṣ	(bu*sh*el)
ṝ	(*rrr*ig)	j	(*J*ohn)	dh	(*d*umb)	s	(*s*o)
ḷ	⎰ no	jh	(*j*am)	n	(*n*umb)	h	(*h*um)
	⎟ English	ñ	(bu*n*ch)	p	(s*p*in)	ṁ	(nasaliza-
	⎟ equiva-	ṭ	⎰ no	ph	(*p*in)		tion of
	⎱ lent	ṭh	⎟ English	b	(bu*n*)		preceding
e	(pl*ay*)		⎟ equiva-	bh	(ru*b*)		vowel)
ai	(h*igh*)		⎱ lent			ḥ	(aspira-
o	(t*oe*)						tion of
au	(c*ow*)						preceding
							vowel)

For information contact:
Chinmaya Mission West
P.O. Box 129
Piercy, CA 95587
(707) 247-3488